Bob Cotner tells us of his pilgrimage from his easy, youthful faith to his hard-won and more reasoned faith of age. What emerges as he recounts his good and interesting life is how the kindness of others, a life of rigorous learning, and a dedication to the joy of poetry have become the centerpieces of his spiritual journey. In a time when politicians and fundamentalists have subverted major religions for their own political gain throughout the world, Cotner's book offers a spiritual corrective.

LAUREL CHURCH
Poet
Professor Emeritus, and Artist in Residence (ret.)
Aurora University

From a small Indiana town and a home where the only book was the Bible, Bob Cotner has become one of the country's best thinkers. He shares his life and his thoughts with us in his first book, *Pilgriming - A Journey Into Faith of Age*. It's hard to realize that this skinny little kid—whom I have known for almost 70 years—has become something of a "Koheleth" in our time, creating a book in the tone and vision of *Ecclesiastes*—his favorite Old Testament book. But he has, and I believe you will enjoy reading as much as I have, *Pilgriming - A Journey Into the Faith of Age*. This may be one of the "wisdom" books for our age.

DAVID H. KLEIMAN
Lifelong Friend
Attorney, Dann Pecar Newman Talesnick & Kleiman
Indianapolis

Pilgriming – A Journey Into the Faith of Age is a spiritual travelogue, one man's journey from the reflexive faith of youth to a more troubled but immensely richer faith of age. Robert Cotner is a committed Christian and a committed humanist, a believer and a scholar, whose quest for understanding takes him into the company and minds of other pilgrims, from Robert Frost to the Nobel physicist Leon Lederman. In an age that digs a moat between religion and scholarship, Bob has spent his life crossing that moat. *Pilgriming* tells us what he found. This is a moving and deeply informed book, a gift to seekers everywhere.

R.C. LONGWORTH
Author, Caught in the Middle: America's
Heartland in the Age of Globalism (2008)
Senior Writer, Chicago Tribune (ret.)

Pilgriming

Pilgriming

A Journey Into The Faith Of Age

Robert Cotner

Tate Publishing *& Enterprises*

Published by Tate Publishing & Enterprises, LLC
127 E. Trade Center Terrace | Mustang, Oklahoma 73064 USA
1.888.361.9473 | www.tatepublishing.com

Tate Publishing is committed to excellence in the publishing industry. The company reflects the philosophy established by the founders, based on Psalm 68:11,
"The Lord gave the word and great was the company of those who published it."

Book design copyright © 2008 by Tate Publishing, LLC. All rights reserved.
Cover design by Kandi Evans
Interior design by Kellie Southerland

Published in the United States of America

ISBN: 978-1-60462-894-4
1. Christian Living: Practical Life: General   2. Philosophy: Religion and Political
08.04.02

To Norma Jean
Constant Companion
Forever Friend

Acknowledgements

Writing is a solitary business. But an author comes to and leaves the keyboard surrounded by friends and colleagues. Permit me to express my appreciation to some of them. First and foremost, are the Reverends Carl Gray and Bart Roush of the Fox Valley Presbyterian Church, who permitted me to teach this book—and thus forced me to *finish* it—in a Wednesday evening adult education class in the church.

Then I must thank the patient people who came for seven weeks to talk about the book, offer suggestions, and share in fellowship of the intellect around the conference table. These include: Wynn and Marilyn Church, Joyce and Tom Egan, Carole and Ken

Hammer, Harrison Schneider, Carol and Ken Seidel, and Guila and Carl Zeigler.

I have had several readers, who have kindly offered comments, suggestions, corrections, and encouragement. These—all friends and intellectual compatriots—include: Barbara Ballinger, Laurel Church, David Kleiman, R.C. Longworth, Steven Masello, the late Carolyn Quattrocchi, and Frederick Turner.

Notice must be made of my friends of the Caxton Club of Chicago, who permitted me to found the *Caxtonian* in 1993 and edit the journal between 1993 and 2004. Several portions of the chapters in this book came from my essays in the *Caxtonian*. They, and many others, are available on the Caxton website, at caxtonclub@newberry.org.

My family, of course, has been integral to the journey into the faith of age and all have read the manuscript and commented upon it. Son Jon Cotner, in North Oaks, Minnesota, and daughter Erin Stuedemann, in Marseilles, Illinois, offered important suggestions. And, of course, wife Norma Jean has been through the rigors of this long journey—and stuck with me, I am thankful to say. She has been an astute critic and commentator, as well as my always-present partner.

To all these people as well as the special people mentioned in the text—church folk, teachers, and friends, out of my past, now no longer present for my expression of gratitude—I say thanks in a solemn way to their memories and to their families still living.

I must express much gratitude toward Annabelle and Blaine Cotner, my parents, who, in the Depression and post-Depression eras reared me in a home filled with laughter and much joy and where anger was always a stranger. An only child, who spent much of his early years alone, I was never lonely.

It's been a marvelous journey, and I remain eternally grateful!

Robert Cotner
Aurora, Illinois
January 1, 2008

Table of Contents

A Foreword

"The Pilgrim's Tale"
Frederick Turner
Founders Professor
Humanities and Arts
University of Texas, Dallas

Bismarck is reputed to have remarked that God protects fools, drunkards, and the United States of America. One of the ways he does so, I believe, is by giving us Americans who are so much better than we deserve. Now, as we approach yet another bitter, rancorous, and abusive national election, we hear from a man who is utterly individual, no fence-sitter or trimmer, but who bridges in his warm and generous way so many of the divisions in our society.

He is a liberal and a conservative—a "radical moderate" as he calls himself. He is a passionate believer in both science and religion. He is a Christian and a humanist. He seems forever young but epitomizes the wisdom of age. He resolves in himself the ancient battle between philosophy and poetry. He is Protestant in his transcendence of dogma and Catholic in his love of art. He is for both word and flesh.

Meet Robert Cotner, an American who for me—a naturalized citizen of this nation—represents the best of my adopted home. A teacher, indefatigable philanthropist, and cultural agitator in the Midwest, a family man, a friend to many, a sort of cracker-barrel philosopher in the tradition of Franklin, Twain, and Thoreau, he offers us a uniquely American wisdom. Part of that uniqueness is, paradoxically, its genuine and deep commitment to the whole human race—his wide acquaintance with many cultures and subcultures is not a departure from Americanness but the very soul of it.

Cotner calls himself a pilgrim, and the deep metaphor of his genial testimony is that life is a journey. Like Chaucer, he meets many different people on his journey and tells their stories. And a grand story emerges, which is about the maturing of a religious man. When we were young we saw religion as a sort of metaphysical superstructure of rules and definitions and abstractions—either as a believer in it, or, in my case, an unbeliever.

The faith of age, as Cotner puts it (nicely reversing the Age of Faith while keeping its spirit) is different.

The life of faith is simply the coming to recognize the truth of what is most valuable. There are, we find, things that ought to be true even if they aren't. And we should act as if they were true, for to live that way is best for us, our fellow-humans, and the world. That "as if," as we mature, comes to be recognized as the secret spirit that enlivens all human life—the subjunctive that opens up possible futures, that conditional mood that gives us responsibility for our own actions, that hiatus in the rush from cause to effect that constitutes our living present.

If we are of a scientific cast of mind, as Cotner is, we begin to recognize in the waywardness of the quantum world and in the amazing branchiness of all the living species of the world the same openness to the future that we sense in the "as if." And so we see the freedom and responsibility we prize in human morality as distributed, perhaps in simpler and more rudimentary forms, throughout the universe.

If we look at the universe's astonishing capacity to grow itself and cause itself, we might reflect that nature every moment becomes something it has never been before. Nature literally becomes supernatural—beyond what nature previously was—in every moment. Nothing is more natural than the supernatural. Nature is, so to speak, the very process of supernaturing. And if we consider this observation from a theological point of view, and ask what might God's purpose be in originating a world which has so thoroughly taken on its own internal power to create futures, we get some surprising answers—answers expressed by Cotner in a much clearer and more straightforward way than in my own lumbering academic explanation.

Taking evolution to be true, as Cotner and I believe it is, then God, if he set it originally in motion by the peculiar suite of universal constants that prevails in this universe, must have valued two things above all. The first is freedom—the freedom of the world to determine its own destiny. That freedom, though, is not always the choice of one alternative as opposed to another, but most characteristically the choice of both possible branches—as Cotner says, "both-and" rather than "either-or." A universe that makes room for and embraces all paths of being is one that is essentially a loving one in itself. And as we see in the science of ecology, and the marvelous consilience of all forms of existence and scientific laws of nature, the continued existence of everything is mutually supporting, mutually enabling. As the Buddhists say, the world comes to be through a continuing process of interdependent co-emergence. Two principles, then, freedom and love, inform Cotner's gentle story. God embraces us, but lets us go. If God is a father, we know that the chief purpose of a father is to have his child grow up to make his own decisions, and there is no greater love than that.

In what I like to call the highbrow gutter press, Baptists are often portrayed like the degenerate, gap-toothed, tobacco-chewing, Appalachian yokels of movies like *Inherit the Wind* and *Deliverance*. Cotner shows what a highly cultured Baptist is like, and it looks pretty good—certainly an example to the jittery, anxious, often angry, and self-loathing bicoastal intellectuals who fly over Cotner's country with a certain distaste for landing there. Emerson, Thoreau, Melville, Hawthorne, Henry Adams, William and Henry James, and Charles Sanders Peirce all came out of the Puritan culture of the Northeast. Cotner shows us what might come out of the analogous Christian culture of the Midwest.

Introduction

Do you remember that dramatic episode in *The Odyssey*, when the wily Odysseus, in his engagement with the Cyclops, is asked, "Who are you?" and declares, "My name is Nobody!"?[1]

That's the name I go by.

All of us, if honest, would confess to that identity, for, in the scheme of things human and historical, we're generally unimportant—real Nobodies. And yet we live with this pervasive metaphor: We strive to be Somebody—a name identified, an achiever recognized, a hero or heroine celebrated. But, for the most part, we live quietly, singularly, and unheralded. And we rejoice through our quiet ways in the private glories composing lives well lived.

One of my private glories is the natural landscape—the vast plowed fields of central Illinois, prepared for seeding and cultivation. A line from a sonnet by my old friend, Jesse Stuart, often comes to mind as I drive through the undulating landscape along Highway 71 between Yorkville and Ottawa, Illinois: "The land is left a scroll for winds to read."[2] Another of my private glories lies in the minutia of the floral panoramas of roadsides, fields, and gardens. I came to love the tuft of spring flowers found on a private hike around Bixler Lake, near my home in Kendallville, Indiana. And I find the incredible blue of the Midwestern summer sky, reflected in lakes and streams, of particular pleasure, and I think often of some lines of a poem by another of my old friends, Philip Appleman:

> that once upon a time we had
> meadows here, and astonishing things,
> swans and frogs and luna moths
> and blue skies that could stagger your
> heart.[3]

My love of nature became directed during my first year in college, 1954, at Taylor University, in a Botany class taught by Vida Wood. (Can you imagine a better-named botany professor than *Vida Wood*!) Miss Wood was among the five finest professors I ever had. And I shall never forget in that first Botany class, walking with her along the back roads of central Indiana in the spring. She carried a notebook and newsprint in a shoulder satchel, and, as we walked, she would spot a choice wild flower, kneel beside it saying its Latin name, and then gather it into her satchel to take back to the laboratory for further identification and for pressing.

And then there was a secluded place not far from campus called "Botany Glen," where Miss Wood would take us for a day's trip to study plant taxonomy. I still have the collection of pressed plants from Botany Glen and the Indiana roadsides—and I continue adding to that collection as I teach my grandchildren the joys of nature.

Much to Miss Wood's regret, I became an English, rather than a biology, teacher. But I found in the study of American literature a rich reference of thinking and writing regarding nature. One thinks, of course, of Ralph Waldo Emerson and Henry David Thoreau, of whom I am a constant student and a lifelong disciple. But other writers, as well, expressed touching insight into the memoirs of nature. I think, in particular, of a passage from Thornton Wilder's marvelous play, *Our Town*. This play was the first major drama I directed in my high school teaching career, and I shall never forget the splendid sentence by Emily from the grave in Act III: "Oh, earth, you're too wonderful for anyone to realize you!"[4] That line, in a very special way, provides a thesis for this classic American play, and is one of many ideas that makes the play so poignant generation after generation.

And so you've guessed by now that my third private glory is literature!

I found in the study of literature, as I had found in the encounters with nature, an intellectual engagement so satisfying, encompassing, and enlightening as to be what I have come to understand as the essence of spiritual perspicacity. And, like Walt Whitman, I understand poetry to be the major universal bond that holds people together as an intellectual entity. Our time is similar, in many ways, to Whitman's time, when strong factions have claimed absolute authority and war against one another, diminishing civil dialogue in the course of their public ranting.

But it is *literature* that binds us as a people; it enunciates our common and universal heritage; it clarifies the humanness—the humanity—of our species. And as one grows older and delves more deeply into the texts and traditions of our literary heritage—expanding wonderfully as new peoples and new literatures are added to the mix—we find a salubrious engagement with thoughts, ideas, and concepts, further linking us and, if we're very lucky, *binding* us as a people.

Overriding all, of course, is the substance of faith, which, if it has any meaning at all, becomes an evolving entity explaining and enriching encounters of all kinds. I understand my particular faith to be best expressed in three distinct metaphors, representative of particular times in my life. In my younger years, faith was a warm and soft, multi-colored quilt, which enfolded all. In my middle years, faith became a rich and colorful robe, which I wore publicly, often with great pride. In my later years, faith is a synapse, that electrical charge, which links neurons within the human body providing for a harmony of movement, function, and understanding.

D. Elton Trueblood, the brilliant Quaker scholar and teacher, was my mentor many years ago—another lifetime, it now seems. I last saw Dr. Trueblood on April 27, 1987. I had arranged for him to speak to the faculty and students of Aurora University, Aurora, Illinois, where I was then vice president. This was his last public speaking engagement before retiring to Landsdale, Pennsylvania, in 1988. I had arranged the benches in Quaker fashion, around the interior of the chapel. Trueblood always sat on a facing bench, surrounded by participants. Andrew Bagnato covered his lecture for the *Chicago Tribune*.

In his talk to Aurora students, he was critical of higher education. "You can easily get through college and not have one big idea," he said. "How sad it makes me feel," he continued, "that millions of people have never read one word [by great thinkers]. They could any time, but they fill their minds with that awful trash in the daily newspapers … most of it worth absolutely nothing. We go for the shallow and the temporary," he concluded, "and miss the greatness."[5]

He finished his talk by quoting the final stanza of Alfred Lord Tennyson's "Ulysses." I told him as we left the chapel how much I appreciated his use of that particular poem, long a favorite of mine. He stopped, turned to me, put an index finger against my chest, and in his stern manner said, "Memorize it!" I did, and I recite it often when I speak in public.

I choose to use it as an invitation to *Pilgriming*, for it comes from the rich depth of the Classical and Victorian traditions of literature. The lines invite the reader to a journey full of dangers and difficulties—not unlike the journey of faith demands, if we are to fulfill it into maturity. In the poem, the aged Ulysses invites his compatriots to join him in yet another voyage:

> Come, my friends,
> 'Tis not too late to seek a newer world.
> Push off, and sitting well in order smite
> The sounding furrows; for my purpose holds
> To sail beyond the sunset, and the baths
> Of all the western stars, until I die.
> It may be the gulfs will wash us down;
> It may be we shall touch the Happy Isles,

And see the great Achilles, whom we knew.
Though much is taken, much abides;
   and though
We are not now that strength which in
   old days
Moved earth and heaven, that which we
   are, we are,
One equal temper of heroic hearts,
Made weak by time and fate, but strong in will
To strive, to seek, to find, and not to yield.[6]

My invitation is similar: Join me on a journey into the faith of age. It will not be easy, and you may, at times, disagree with what I say. But bear with me, and you will find new horizons, new experiences, and new worlds—all of which will enrich your life in ways totally unexpected.

And so I say at the beginning of this journey: *Come, my friends ...*

The Faith of Age

I am an old man in Christ.

I was baptized in the First Baptist Church in Kendallville, Indiana, nearly 60 years ago. It beats me why they called our church the "First" Baptist Church; it was the *only* Baptist Church. But, I suppose to call it the "Only Baptist Church" would have frightened them. Nobody in those days wanted to be the *only* of anything, even though, I have learned, to become an *only* in life is what we're really all about.

Indeed, it is an integral part of our American heritage to pursue our *only* throughout life. It is what Ralph Waldo Emerson and Henry David Thoreau urged us toward. It is what Walt Whitman, Emily Dickinson, Wallace Stevens, Robert Frost, and others fulfilled in lives of poetic creation. This *only* becomes what critic Harold Bloom calls "genius," which he defines and elaborates on so beautifully in his splendid book *Genius.*[1] In the introduction, Bloom reminds us, "Our desire for the transcendental and extraordinary seems part of our common heritage, and abandons us slowly, and never completely."[2]

It has not abandoned me even though, following my baptism, I became one of the finest disciples of the Baptist church anywhere. I had read the Bible completely through for the first time by the time I was 18. Throughout high school I was a bible-thumping evangelical, and everyone knew it.

I went to an evangelical college and married an evangelical young woman, and we have had two evangelical children. As I matured (ever so slowly, it now seems) I tried my hardest to remain in the evangelical camp. The churches we chose to attend, the friends we cultivated, the cultural activities in which we participated, and the things we did *not* do marked me as a "Christian."

More than 20 years ago, while sitting at worship in a United Methodist Church in a small community in central Indiana, I had an epiphany: "You don't belong here, Cotner," my inner voice told me. "These people think in an either-or fashion—you think in a both-and manner." I didn't fully understand the implications of that conversation at the time.

Dava Sobel, in her remarkable book, *Galileo's*

Daughter,[3] helped me toward a greater understanding. This book is a dual biography of the great Renaissance scientist and thinker, Galileo Galilei, and his daughter, Suor Marie Celeste, a Sister of the Poor Clare in the San Matteo convent in Arcetri. Through a discovered collection of letters from Suor Marie to her father, we come to know religious devotion in its most sublime form, and we find insight into the most creative years of Galileo.

But the most important, though I believe unintentional, dimension of the book is the delineation of two distinct faiths: The Faith of Youth and the Faith of Age. The Faith of Youth is elegantly simple and very powerful. It is comprehensive, confident, and efficacious. Emanating from, I might suggest, the "trailing clouds of glory,"[4] to use Wordsworth's words, it perfects private piety through devotion, discipline, and allegiance. With sufficient virtue to carry each through extraordinarily difficult years, in due time, it brings the believer to maturity.

The Faith of Age, on the other hand, is inordinately complex. It is anchored in what is ultimate, fulfilling through wisdom, courage, and love, the highest enterprises of which human beings are capable. Because it exists on the extremities of what can be known, a certain tentativeness is inherent in this faith. But the consummate explorations for a greater common good by a searching, mature soul holds the possibility of carrying humankind into emerging, yet-to-be understood, realms.[5]

What I had been seeking—what many, as they move into maturity, seek—was an exposition of the Faith of Age.

The Residual Elements from the Faith of Youth

I am tempted to say that progress in life begins with a state of unself-consciousness in early youth, proceeds to a state of extreme self-consciousness in adolescence through middle age, and returns to a new unself-consciousness in old age. But it is more than that. We have the potential of developing a comprehensive "life of the mind," to borrow from Hannah Arendt's splendid book of that title, in which she proposes three activities of the mind: Thinking, Willing, and Judging. In the development of the life of the mind, we learn, as Arendt did from St. Augustine, that "Love is a kind of enduring and conflictless Will." She comes to this marvelous understanding: "Love is the soul's gravity."[6]

As we grow older in grace and move more deeply into maturity, there is a falling away of external manifestations of the faith. The concern for the "things" of faith become less and less important; the concern for inner dimensions, deeper personal relationships, and sounder linkages with those elements bearing marks of the eternal on them become more intent.

The life of the soul in age is a life of passionate human love—the weight of love becomes very great—and profound intellectual engagement. We do in age what we lacked sufficient understanding and courage to do in youth. I think of a personal relationship I formed in 1988, when I assumed a leadership role as a civilian in the Chicago division of the Salvation Army. In the staff of twenty-five, I assumed direction of a young man just coming from the Harbor Light program in Chicago, the program for drug and alcohol rehabilitation. The man had been a Ph. D. candidate in Oriental Studies at the University of Chicago before the necessity of entering the Harbor Light program arose. He was bright, eager, and had sufficiently recovered from his alcoholism. We talked frequently, and he was so enthusiastic to be in the workforce and free from drinking.

We worked well together for six months, when, suddenly, he disappeared, and no one knew where he was. Some days passed and, finally, I had a call from a motel operator on the South Side of Chicago; my man was in his room, drunk. I drove down to the motel and retrieved him, taking him to the Veterans hospital for drying out. This was the first of three incidents in which I went to a YMCA or motel to help him to my car and transport him to the VA hospital for treatment. He and

I grieved together over his inability to remain sober for any length of time. One of the final incidents occurred during a rainstorm. A neighbor called to tell me he was lying in the mud in a tomato patch and couldn't get up. I went to the garden, helped him to his feet—thoroughly soaked, drunk, and miserable—and, nearly as muddy as he was, I took him to the VA hospital.

This story does not have a happy ending. In 1992, having left the Army completely and taken on other enterprises of which he was capable, for a time, to fulfill, he went into a deep drunk and died of cirrhosis of the liver at the age of 49.

There are other stories, but this one will suffice as illustrative. The most important residual element of the faith of youth into the faith of age is a consummate, abiding, and unconditional love of people. I once had a Baptist friend who claimed that the imprint of God on the life of an individual in youth is inescapable as we age; that we are forever marked by the stamp of God's presence in our lives. It becomes a condition, as we mature, which seems both ever present and comprehensive. I fully understand why Walt Whitman went to minister to the Civil War wounded. Harold Bloom writes of Whitman, one of America's true geniuses:

> heroic wound-dresser and unpaid male nurse in the hospitals of Washington,

> D.C....There is no comparable figure of
> such authentic compassionate heroism
> in our literary culture, and our image of
> Whitman forever is fixed as "the brother
> angel" of the study by Roy Morris, Jr., who
> says that this apotheosis "saved" Whitman
> as a person.

Whitman's own Quaker upbringing seemed to be inescapable for him in his later years. Bloom extends this idea, saying, "If there is an American Christ, then here he is in 'The Wound-Dresser.'"[7]

The task, as I see it from my seventieth year, is to extend through kindness, humor, critical intelligence, and ultimate concern the love of God. He has no feet but ours, no voice but ours, and no helping hands but ours. We have no purpose but to serve the high and the low of our society, acting as a leaven in the mass, altering by subtlety, gentleness, and firmness the social fabric, torn by competition, strife, and malice.

Lines of Whitman's *Leaves of Grass* come to mind:

> I am he bringing help for the sick as they
>   pant on their backs,
> And for the strong upright men I bring yet
>   more needed help.
> I heard what was said of the universe,

Heard it and heard it of several thousand years;
It is middling well as far as it goes—but is
    that all?[8]

I ask with Whitman regarding what has been said of the universe, "but is that all?" It is not. The call of faith is a call that echoes across hills and valleys, over rivers and seas, through years and lives. It is not singular but plural of plurals. And in plurality we find common consent to sing, to weep, to laugh, to celebrate in diversity the universal heritage of the human soul.

Families in the Scheme of Love

This plurality may best be found in the family. I think of my wife's family, for example, which carries a story for the ages in its history. When my wife Jeanne was ten years old, her parents, chronic alcoholics, decided they did not want their eight children any longer and made arrangements to give them away. The three older ones—Jeanne was the second oldest—were taken in by the maternal grandparents. The remaining children were offered for adoption. Jeanne yet remembers with almost unbearable personal pain, when, at the tender age of ten, she held her six-month-old sister Kathy in her arms awaiting the arrival of strangers to take her away. Little Eddie, crying, stood by Jeanne's side, awaiting his new parents.

The three oldest, remaining with the grandparents, came to know the aunts, uncles, and cousins within the family. But the others were gone, forever lost, they thought, from the sweet pleasures of family life among one another. One sister, Delores, was adopted by a neighboring family, and the four siblings, as they grew older, determined to find and, if possible, restore their relationships. Their love, though not nurtured by normal family associations, burned brightly, and, as this love matured, the four children who remained close sought to find their lost brothers and sisters.

Eddie tells this story: He had been adopted by a family some forty miles from the original family home. Ten years after the family's split, Jeanne's engagement to me was announced in a newspaper with a photo of my wife-to-be. Eddie saw the photo, took it to his adoptive mother, and told her, "I love that girl." She looked at the picture, recognized Jeanne's family name, and said, "Eddie, that's your sister." Eddie was the first to be restored to the family circle. Just two years ago, after fifty years of separation, Kathy met the sister who held her at six months, as Kathy was restored to the circle. One by one, the lost children were found and became family again.

On September 28, 2007, the last family member was joined to the original group. Hank, who had been told by his adoptive parents that he was an only child, was reunited with his seven original brothers and sisters, and they sang "Happy Birthday" to him for his sixty-fourth birthday. His wife wryly asked him, "Did you think a year ago, Hank, that you'd be sung to on your sixty-fourth birthday by a bunch of brothers and sisters?"

On October 15, 2007, Delores, who had been a major force in bringing the family together, died. And the family gathered again, at her funeral. Her sister Jeanne, my wife, gave the family eulogy, saying of Delores: "Your mission was accomplished. Now there was our reunited family: Mary, Jeanne, Nate, Delores, Eddie, Hank, Kathy, and Suzanne." It was one of those joyously sad occasions that mark certain significant events in everyone's life.

Sixty years after the disintegration of the family, the siblings had come together in their own unique, loving community. The seven remaining siblings correspond regularly by email, telephone, and letter, and get together in person at least once a year. It is testimony to the power of maturing love and the determination of children that their family relationship is intact as maturing adults. It is one of the beautiful stories of restoration of family against great odds.

Families that do not experience the grief of separation through divorce or other violent causes are more fortunate. As children mature, marry, and have their own families, the richness of love abounds and matures in the aging process. Our own two children, nurtured in the faith of youth as young people, have grown into maturity as balanced adults. Well educated and married to mates who are equally mature, they have brought into our lives other families—the in-laws—who have increased the diversity of joy, pleasure, and, of course, sadness. Two in-law parents have died, and we have been touched by the grief shared by all.

But the greatest pleasure of mature love lies in grandparenting. To meet and come to love a new generation of the family in the children of our children is beyond description in beauty and satisfaction. I have decided to have a new business card printed. It will say, "Robert Cotner, g. b." What does "g. b." stand for, you asked? Why anyone would know—"Grandpa Bob!" No more noble title is possible, it now seems to me, than *Grandpa Bob*.

There is an extraordinary metaphor in the writing of Robert Frost. In 1925, he wrote:

> The most exciting movement in nature is not progress, advance, but expansion and contraction, the opening and shutting of the eye, the hand, the heart, the mind. We throw our arms wide with a gesture of religion to the universe; we close them around a person. We explore and adventure for a while and then we draw in to consolidate our gains.[9]

Frost's metaphor of the opening arms is a perfect description of the most mature love: We open our arms wide, draw others to us, but always let them go—as go they must in time. We hold and release the aging parent, to whom we become surrogate parent. We hold for a time the child who grows up and leaves home. We hug and then yield the grandchild whom we shall never see in fulfillment. All are held and released. But the holding as an act of love is so urgent, for through it, we imbue with the strength of love and care those whom it is our pleasure to know intimately.

There is another important entity, and that is the family of faith we discover in our church or through our religious affiliations. If we're fortunate, we find a community of thinking, loving, active believers, and we open our arms to them in this universal gesture of love, peace, and fellowship.

This book was read, deliberated upon, and refined by a group of eleven parishioners in the Fox Valley Presbyterian Church, Geneva, Illinois. My mentor, D. Elton Trueblood, held that a book should be taught before it is published. So, before being prepared for publication, *Pilgriming* was read and discussed thoroughly, chapter-by-chapter, by a volunteer group, and both they and I risked greatly in joining together for seven weeks to learn what the "Faith of Age" is all about, and whether this expression of that faith was worthy of print. The book is better for our dialogue. And we enjoyed the weekly considerations into the grandness of the human enterprise as believing peoples. We did not all agree on every detail, but we had pleasure in discussion—and became best friends in the process.

I live differently from how I lived twenty-five years ago, thirty-five years ago, and fifty years ago. It is not the prerogatives of the times that dictate my life; it is, rather, the persuasion of my mind in its maturing years to forge from yesterday's dreams, today's realities. It is through the sacred scripture, so much a part of my life over the years, but it is more, much more. It is through the distillation of thoughts and ideas gleaned from every venue of intellect, from all disciplines of learning, and from the subtle involvement of a spiritual reality in my intellectual life that is more real and more powerful as I grow in years and stature.

This is not, of course, just a personal aspiration; we deal in great social issues emanating from the single heart, from the community spirit of faith and society. I think of a stanza from the great American hymn, "God of Grace and God of Glory," by Harry Emerson Fosdick, which elucidates through the poetry of the hymn precisely what I mean:

> Cure thy children's warring madness;
> Bend our pride to thy control;
> Shame our wanton, selfish gladness,

Rich in things and poor in soul.
Grant us wisdom, grant us courage,
Lest we miss thy kingdom's goal.
Lest we miss thy kingdom's goal. [10]

I believe it possible for a people to miss completely the "Kingdom's goal." I believe the focus in churches on parishioner's being "children of God" rather than "men and women of God" diminishes the sense of responsibility, which all adults must accept to insure the growth of their faith into its most comprehensive stature and to strengthen their communities of faith, responsible for encouraging growth and providing fellowship of maturing people. I believe the emphasis on elementary, repetitious aspects of liturgy and scripture render people of faith into talking heads—even mere puppets. I believe that the turning away from the available, current literature of wisdom—secular and sacred (if there is a difference)—and refusing to reconcile that literature, where possible, with scripture cultivates the superficiality of intellect that is destroying both current and future prospects for the faith. Such a turning away makes people shrill and shallow, as many identified with religions of all kinds have become in these days.

In short, the task of *pilgriming* is urgent in our day—for ourselves, for our children, and for children unborn, who will be blessed by a deepening of the faith into a profound understanding of human life, of learning, and of God himself.

Growing up in a Jewish Home

I grew up in a Jewish home.

Now don't misunderstand me—I was *reared* a Baptist, but as a neighborhood urchin with no brothers and sisters, I was, until 16 years of age, a part of the extended household of a neighborhood friend, David, and he was Jewish.

David and I were best friends when friendship was the coin of the realm. As the only kids in the neighborhood our age, we played two-man football—I was Glenn Davis and he, "Doc" Blanchard (or was it the other way around?)—and two-man baseball. In the winter, we sledded, had snowball fights, and then went indoors to play caroms or Monopoly when we got cold.

David was in my wedding in 1956, and we attended

his at Chicago's Blackstone Hotel in 1957. During his sixtieth birthday dinner at the Columbia Club, Indianapolis, a while back, I was proud to have him introduce me as his "oldest friend"—though "friend of longest standing" might have been just a tad better.

David's father, Isadore, who had come from Chicago to our town in the 1920s to open a junkyard, was the first reader of books I knew. Evenings, I'd always see him stretched out in a living room chair, feet on a hassock, reading. I picked up the habit of reading early in life in great measure because of Isadore.

Abraham Wicoff, David's grandfather, who was co-owner of a dairy in Chicago, drove the 150 miles to our town occasionally. Seeing his battered '38 Buick sedan in front of David's house always pleased me because I enjoyed "Grandpa," and he had taken a liking to me as well. A diminutive man with a broad smile, he spoke an English I could never fully understand. David's mother Pearl, a lovely, gracious woman, always served as interpreter on my behalf.

I remember Grandpa's one visit in particular, when I was about ten years old. Greeting me in the living room, he excused himself and came back shortly carrying a small box. Pearl came into the room as if prearranged, and Grandpa handed me the box, which I immediately opened. Inside was a scroll of the *Torah* in a pink silk cover. "Grandpa brought this special gift to you from Chicago,"

Pearl interpreted. I ran home to show my mother, working in the kitchen. I have kept the *Torah* for more than sixty years in a dresser drawer reserved for special items. As I think of it now, this *Torah* is my first collectible "book" and remains one of my most cherished.

On December 30, 1986, my mother called to tell me Isadore had died, and his funeral was to be in Chicago that day. I cancelled my schedule and went to the funeral. Even in that solemn setting, there was much joy as dear friends met after more than thirty years. We then went to Waldheim Cemetery, where I saw the family burial plot, including the grave of Abraham Wicoff.

All this is to say that real growing up, true maturity, comes, it seems to me, as we learn to understand and accept at least one other culture, including another religion, as equal to our own. Perhaps only as we find cultural equality can we achieve equality of the individual. These were my thoughts as I returned to Isadore's grave the day following his funeral just to contemplate his significance in my life. I wrote an elegy in his memory, for his family and for myself. It became my gift, an exchange for the miniature *Torah* and the blessed bond of friendship it represents—across years, miles, and cultures.[1]

In a Jewish Cemetery Near Chicago
In Memory of Isadore Kleiman

A rabbit, startled by my step, darts from
    cover to cover,
across the cluttered landscape and disappears
    between leaning stones.
Overhead, a single squirrel performs winter
    ritual on black branches;
a broken twig falls, marking the snowy
    mound of turned sod,
where yesterday we planted memory—as
    crows circled in the south,
their plaintive calls mingled with the gloom
    and quiet grieving here.
"The heart of the wise dwells in the house of
    mourning." I thought.

This is an ancient place—once remote from
    city noise and soil;
it lies along hissing streets that glisten
    toward the lake—
as far from New Year's Day as psalms and
    prayers.
Above the ashen clouds today, jetliners settle
    into laser lanes

and make their whistling ways from sun
    through cloud
to earth, dispatching harried souls along
    their paths,
from cover to cover. Only death gives pause
    for contemplation.

You, Old Friend, now settle into the shape
    of eternity,
fashioned these four-score years far from
    here among folks
whose names ring foreign to this place. You
    are home now,
among Bonners, Cohens, Ecksteins,
    Mendelssohns, and Wicoffs.
Stranger in this land, you lived apart and
    knew the solemn
satisfaction of solitude among noisy people.
    You found the Law
a river nourishing mind toward deeds of
    private grace.

They are scattered now—the children and
    grandchildren; the wife,
who left remembering, "Two are better than
    one, … " the friends,

who stood impatient and cold to hear the
    final prayer,
to watch family spade dirt on vault. So I
    returned, to praise
the dead who are already dead more than the
    living are alive.
There is kinship beyond reticence and ritual.
    Sojourners find
one another pleasant company here. How
    strange it seems.

New Year's Day, 1987

An acceptance of another's religion as an equal to
one's own is something that comes with maturity. I
could not have admitted that truth when I was younger.
I now know that the working faith in each of us is both
peculiar and sufficient unto itself. There was an inherent
understanding I had about my faith as a young person
that told me if I invited David to my church, all manner
of effort would have been brought to bear to convert
him to the Baptist way of thinking. That would have
been embarrassing for both of us, and I never invited
him to church with me—though best friends we were
and though the church was so important in my life.

One day when teaching in a college in suburban
Washington, DC, a number of years ago, I told my students that my business card said on it, "Robert Cotner,

h. b." What does "h. b." stand for, they asked. "Human Being!" Nothing else matters, I told them—not degrees, not nationality, not race, not religion. "We've got to learn to see each other, simply, as *human beings*, and nothing else."

I recently read Pat Conroy's moving novel, *Beach Music*,[2] the story of a young Jewish woman who had grown up in a Southern town about the time that David and I were growing up in the Midwest. In the novel, Jewish families living in America came to know that something dreadful was happening in Europe during World War II, for, without explanation, correspondence with European relatives ceased, and word began circulating about the Holocaust. I called David when I finished the novel to tell him about it. I asked David if his family had heard during World War II from any of their relatives living in Europe what was happening to Jewry at the hands of the Nazi Germans. To his knowledge, they had not heard, but, he said, they really didn't talk much about things like that in those days.

Knowing David's generously kind parents, I judged that they would have kept any knowledge of this great tragedy—which no one where we lived could do anything about—from their children, who were their greatest joy and their most important legacy.

I had much pleasure in reading Elisabeth Sifton's splendid book, *The Serenity Prayer*,[3] which focuses on the years in which David and I grew up. This is an important book for our time, for it is concerned with "faith and politics in times of peace and war"—times not unlike those in which we live. The book's significance lies in its expression of harmony existing among people surrounding Sifton's father, pastor, professor, and distinguished theologian, Reinhold Niebuhr. "Some of them," she wrote, "were agnostics or atheists, some of them were Jews, and quite a few of them were Protestant ministers."[4]

In this community of intellectual and spiritual diversity, Niebuhr came into his own very special maturity of faith—one of the products of which was the "Serenity Prayer."

> God, give us grace
> to accept with serenity
> the things that cannot be changed,
> courage to change the things
> that should be changed,
> and the wisdom to distinguish
> the one from the other.

The prayer, written in 1943 by Niebuhr on one of the family's summer retreats in Heath, Massachusetts, was first read at the Union Church there. It was a time of grave concern about the war in Europe. Niebuhr's close personal friend and fellow pastor, Dietrich

Bonhoeffer, Bonhoeffer's brother Klaus, and their brother-in-law were in German prisons—and would shortly be executed.

In the face of such awesome fear and grief, Niebuhr presented in seven lines of poetry a magnificent utterance, later thought to be Old Testament by some, Medieval by others, or Roman Catholic by still others—its grace was so wisely expressed. In the heat of battle, this prayer is calm and peaceful; in the raging anger toward known atrocities, this prayer is gentle and kind; in the elevated environment of Union Seminary, where Niebuhr taught, this prayer is elemental in its language and style. It is one of the great expressions of spirituality of modern times. It is the ultimate expression of serenity of the soul in the midst of circumstances so dreadful as to be, when learned, unbelievable.

Sifton taught me a new word from her father's role as spiritual advisor to the nation in its gravest crisis. It is a word that in my younger years I would not have understood nor used. That word is "philo-Semitism,"[5] and in my growing up years with the Kleiman family, as neighbors and friends, I came to know and understand thoroughly *philo-Semitism*. It is still a strong component in my life, though I confess to an even broader love, which I call *philo-humanism*.

As I mature, I am convinced that the single most important dimension of the human expression is *love*:

"And the greatest of these is [love]" (I Cor. 13:13). Walt Whitman, who taught Americans so powerfully in his *Leaves of Grass*, reminded us of the "cruelties of creeds."[6] Here Whitman spoke of the man-made "creeds" of faith and not the inspired creeds, such as the Nicean or Apostles Creeds, which are legitimate expressions of our living faith. The man-made creeds, established to bring others under the control of religious leaders, are cruel, to their adherents and to those who oppose them, no matter how well intentioned nor seemingly innocent they may seem. It is only as we *leave* our man-made creeds for love of humankind that we find the common bond with the power to truly save—ourselves, our communities, our world. We must move from the letter to the spirit of the Law.

We all have been touched by creeds: Don't to this! Do that! Creeds are indeed the taskmasters of the faith of youth. Creeds have been the driving force in the ministry of people like Jim Jones and David Koresh. We witnessed the ultimate in the cruelty of creeds in Germany under the Nazis, who had a single creed: If you're Jewish, you are disenfranchised, robbed, and murdered. More recently, we have witnessed the horrible cruelty of another creed, which declares all peoples not Muslim as infidels and worthy only of death: the airplane attacks on the Pentagon, World Trade Center Towers, and the Pennsylvania countryside on September 11, 2001, taking

3,000 innocent lives, demonstrated the ultimate cruelty of creeds in recent years. Such deeds emanate from criminal zealotry masquerading as authentic religion.

Toward a Sacred Humanism

We know a better way. We have examples of better ways. Let me tell you one of those ways. It has been my pleasure to work at Shriners Hospitals for Children in Chicago for a number of years. Shriners Hospitals were first created in 1922, in Shreveport, Louisiana, to provide much-needed care for children suffering from infantile paralysis—later know as polio. In the next dozen years, Shriners built three hospitals a year, creating what William Mayo, a Shriner at Mayo Clinic, Rochester, Minnesota, called a "network" of pediatric hospitals. Today, there are 22 Shriners Hospitals in North America, with a combined budget of $780 million annually (2008 budget). Shriners spend two million dollars a day on the welfare of children.

Shriners have expanded their pediatric care to all orthopedic necessities, spinal cord injuries, craniofacial concerns, and burns. They treat more than 120,000 children a year at no charge to the children, their families, healthcare organizations, or the government.

Besides free medical care to treat some of the most serious medical problems known to humankind,

Shriners, through the generosity of their members, provide transportation for children to and from each hospital at no charge. Every day, thousands of Shriners get behind the steering wheels of their Shrine vans, with another Shriner riding "shotgun," and bring patients and their parents to Shriners Hospitals. The *Murat Shrine*, Indianapolis, the nation's largest Shrine center, has 14 vans on the road bringing children from fifty-one Indiana counties to hospitals in Chicago, Cincinnati, Ohio, St. Louis, Missouri, or Lexington, Kentucky.

One *Mizpah* Shriner out of Ft. Wayne, Indiana, has made 825 trips to Shriners Hospitals. In the northern tier of counties of Indiana, 2,000 children are now under the care of Shriners hospitals. Ft. Wayne has six vans in operation regularly, and, on occasion, four of their vans will be at the Chicago hospital on the same day. *Moslem Shrine*, Detroit, Michigan, has an especially designed bus used to transport up to 15 patients and their families at a time from the eastern Michigan area.

Shriners Headquarters estimates that, since 1985, Shrine vans have traveled more than 200 million miles bringing children to and from Shriners hospitals in North America. In addition to the thousands of Shriners traveling to hospitals by vans daily, more than 1,000 Shriners pilot their planes, bringing seriously burned or critically injured children to a Shriners hospital. These pilots fly over a million miles a year—all without charge—to help children in medical crises.

While walking through the Chicago hospital several weeks ago, I met in the hallway a small boy—7 or 8, I should guess—who was struggling down the hallway with a walker. I stopped, leaned over, and said, "You're doing such a fine job!"

He smiled, and his mother, who was standing behind him, said, "This is the first time he has ever walked." Children like this touch my heart.

It was my great pleasure to visit Shriners Hospitals for Children–Galveston, one of the nation's first pediatric burn centers, which opened in 1966. This hospital is closely affiliated with the University of Texas Medical Branch—SHC is, in fact, considered a part of the university campus. I had a rare tour at this hospital. Led by Chief of Staff Dr. David Herndon, I was taken into the treatment center and saw four children who would have died had it not been for SHC–Galveston. Let me say that it is a tour you would not want to take, and yet it is a tour you would not want to *miss* taking in a lifetime. I saw children with burns over ninety percent of their bodies, now stabilized and recovering. I heard of the remarkable work by SHC–Boston, where medical research has led to "artificial skin," to "cultured skin," and to "skin banks," all so important to the recovery of burn patients. I met staff members who daily work with suffering children, badly injured by burns, who, in another time and place, would have been given up to death. I learned of the relationship between Shriners burn centers in Boston, Cincinnati, Galveston, and Sacramento. Thirty years ago, a child with burns over thirty percent of his body would have died. Today, primarily because of the extraordinary pioneering work in burn care by Shriners hospitals, children with burns covering ninety percent of their bodies can be saved.

Nothing that I have experienced in my long life is more humanly compelling than what I witnessed on this tour! Nothing being done for children anywhere in the world is more urgent—and more spiritually beautiful—than the work of Shrine medical doctors, nurses and staff, psychologists, social workers, donors, families, and the team of volunteers who make possible the dramatic medical care provided by Shriners Hospitals for Children on behalf of children injured in ways most gruesome and tragic. The world needs to know the *rarity* and the magnificence of what Shriners are doing in our time for children.

I am reminded of a conversation among four Shrine drivers, who came by my office recently to "shoot the breeze," as they say. They were talking, of course, about kids and the hospitals. Larry, from South Bend, Indiana, said, "I think it ought to be a prerequisite for all Shriners to make at least one trip, *with a child*, to one of our hospitals. It's important," he said, "to have one of the children touch your heart, to understand what the Shrine is all about."

Another said, "I don't know why people join the Shrine if they don't get involved with the hospitals."

Larry told about a mother sitting in the lobby, crying. He asked her if there was something he could do to help. "Oh," she said, "you've already done enough. My daughter just rode a tricycle for the first time, and I just had to have a good cry about it!"

Larry, a large, bald man with a pierced ear—who plays the piano marvelously, then said,

> Let me tell you about a boy from South Bend, who was one of three to survive a terrible house fire. Two others died in the fire. Mark had both his ears burned off and was greatly disfigured. When he was just a little fellow, I was taking him to the Cincinnati burn center, and he was being obstreperous as we drove, and he wouldn't stay in his seat belt. Finally, just east of Indianapolis, I pulled the van off the highway and said, "Look, Friend, either you sit down and fasten your seat belt and keep it fastened, or I'm going to turn this van around and take you back home."

Mark said, "You're serious, aren't you!"

"You bet your bippy, I'm serious! You decide!" Mark never caused a moment's trouble on any trip beyond that time.

That's what touching the heart means!

Larry continued the story: "Mark's grandmother Diane called me one day several years later to tell me Mark was in trouble in school, would I help out. 'What's the problem?' I asked. 'He got kicked out for fighting,' she replied." Larry went to Mark's home and talked with him.

"Why the fight, Mark?" Larry asked him.

"This guy said my face looked like a piece of burned shit, and I lost it—I hit him!"

"I'll tell you what, Mark. I used to love to fight, but it doesn't get you anywhere but in trouble. The next time someone says something like that to you, you tell him, 'Inside, I'm a better person than you on the outside'—and then walk away." It worked, Larry reported.

Another time, Mark called Larry to tell him he wanted "real ears" and not plastic ears. "I want to have my ear pierced like yours," Mark told Larry. The Shriners hospitals now are able to generate new ears from the rib cartilage, and Mark now has real ears—and one of them is pierced, just like Larry's. He's now sixteen years old and a straight-A student in school.[7]

JC, a fighter pilot off an aircraft carrier in the Pacific during World War II—one of the "Flyboys"—didn't say much during the conversation. He sat, listening to others and wiping tears from his eyes as others told their stories of being touched by children. But JC, a driver for *Orak Shrine* out of Michigan City, Indiana, reminded us, as we were leaving, about a sign he had seen on a Shrine trailer in a Tampa parade. It said, "We couldn't decide how much to charge, so we don't." I must confess that this was the best bull session I have had since college days!

And it brings me to this conclusion: True faith is best fulfilled in what I call "sacred humanism." It means wrapping your arms around another person until she can walk on her own, until he has real ears, or until his wounds are thoroughly healed. It is the ultimate concern by people who love people.

THE CALL IS FOR "UNBOUNDED LOVE" FOR CHILDREN—FOR PEOPLE

While working for the Salvation Army in the summer of 1993, when the awesome floods struck the Middle West, I supervised the shipments of goods and foodstuffs from Chicago to fifteen Army centers along the swollen Missouri, Mississippi, and other rivers west of us. We had had excellent television coverage, and, while working one day, I received a call from a man from the Midwest Buddhist Temple, Chicago, asking if I would present a program at the temple the next Sunday about the Army's work along the flooded rivers. I was delighted to do so, and I spoke to both the children and youth of the temple and to the adults in their worship service. In conjunction with this assignment, a verse started coming to my mind, and I wrote "There Is But One Child."

THERE IS BUT ONE CHILD
FOR THE CHILDREN OF
MIDWEST BUDDHIST TEMPLE, CHICAGO

There is but one child,
   and he is all of you.

There is but one child,
   and she is all children
      in the city,
      in the nation,
      in the world.

There is but one child,
   since the first child was born,
   until the last shall pass away.

When that child is happy, the world rejoices,
   in laughter, lightness, expectation.

When that child is injured,
  you suffer;
When that child is abused,
  all children are hurt;
When that child is killed,
  hope for humankind lies murdered.

There is but one child;
  therefore, be kind to yourself;
  understanding of others;
  vigilant for the welfare of all.

When you are parent, rearing your own child,
  know that there is but one child;
  that child is yours,
  and all the world's children depend upon you.

The call in our time must be to mature intellects, committed to unbounded love for humankind, to restore through shared humanism a new wholeness in the scheme of things human. Only as we do this do we have the remote possibility of coming to know and experience in society the peace that "passeth all understanding" (Phil. 4:7) among us as a world people. Through such peace, which I believe to be possible in our time—as people of intellect join together—we shall nullify the hate, bigotry, and violence that have come to characterize these days.

This is the call to *Pilgriming* as this old man of the faith sees it.

On Becoming a
Radical Moderate

I want to introduce Lucille and Rosella.

Please understand that I never called either woman by those names. I called them, as was the custom of the day, *Miz* Hire and *Miz* Kimmel. They were, I suppose you could say, *missionaries* from the First Baptist Church sent forth to rescue folks from the great unchurched mass, among which my family was numbered when the two women arrived on the scene.

I'll never forget the day. I was, I suppose, five or six years old and playing on a summer's day in the front yard of our house on Orchard Street. All of a sudden, this lime-green, 1941 Oldsmobile pulled up and parked in front of our house. I looked up as *Miz* Lucille Hire got out on the driver's side. She was a matronly woman, dressed in pink and wearing a broad-brimmed lacy dress hat, as women in those days did, even on weekdays. *Miz* Rosella Kimmel got out the passenger door. She was a tall woman, wearing dark clothes and a feminine version of a man's dress hat—though a bit taller, with a more stylish rake to it, and worn low over her right eye.

As the women walked up the sidewalk toward our front door, they glanced toward me, smiled, and then mounted the steps to the front porch and knocked on the door. My mother, busy with housework inside, answered the door, and the women disappeared within the living room. They had come, my mother reported at the supper table that evening, to invite her, my father, and me to attend the First Baptist Church. My mother was especially moved by their kindness and their gracious invitation to come to church. My father, who operated a Warner & Swasey turret lathe at the Flint & Walling Manufacturing Company, was skeptical about the prospects of becoming a Baptist, but would rather please my mother than start a fuss. The next Sunday, we began our sojourn within the Baptist church, which would so drastically and sharply define my life, then and into the future.

We became conservative of conservatives. Because of the restrictions of the church, there would be no alcohol in our house, ever—which was no big deal, for my father or mother did not indulge in drinking of any kind. I never saw either of them drink wine or beer throughout their lives. And I never tasted an alcoholic drink until New Year's Eve, 1965, when I was on the faculty of Ball State University, and my wife and I decided to try a bottle of wine for our private New Year's Eve celebration.

And I never saw a movie—you must remember that television didn't come along until the 1950s—until I was fourteen. Then, my friend David had a birthday party at the Strand Theater—and through strategic negotiations on behalf of *Miz* Kleiman with my mother, I was granted one-time permission to attend a movie with David and his friends. We saw "The Deerslayer," and I loved it! In the Cotner house—and in their church—there was no dancing, no card playing, no wildness tolerated of any kind. It made for a pretty quiet childhood and youth!

But it was a pretty tame life all around the town in my early years. Even non-Baptists were fairly conservative in their approach to life in small-town America in those days. We were in the midst of World War II, and all were committed to saving for the war effort. Gasoline and tires were rationed, and travel was thus limited.

And we were poor. We knew nothing of *poverty*— we were just poor—dirt-poor, as the saying goes. To be poor makes you conservative; to be in poverty makes you liberal. And we were *poor*! We didn't own our house—we rented, for $15 a month. We had no automobile. We had no telephone. We had no bathroom and no running water in the house until I was ten years old, and then it was cold water piped into the kitchen. But no one complained. We worked toward a brighter future, which we knew would some day arrive. And, of course, it did. For my family, it came in 1952, when my father and mother bought their first house—for $3,500—and we had our first bathroom and a furnace-heated house. What a joy it was!

I fell in love with school, with learning, and with reading at a early age. Evenings were almost always spent in my growing-up years at the public library and doing homework, which I enjoyed more than anything. I had marvelous English teachers, and I became fond of literature of all kinds, beginning with *Evangeline*, *Ivanhoe*, *The Lady of the Lake*, *Moby Dick*, and the writings of Edgar Alan Poe, Henry David Thoreau, and the whole pantheon of American and English writers. All of these writers were conservative, just like us—or we read them that way.

I must tell you about *Miz* Peachy—that was her real name: Ella Peachy—who attended our Baptist church. She was a short, broad lady, whose head sat squarely upon her shoulders, and she always smiled. She learned early in my church years that I loved poetry. Each Sunday morning, she would await my arrival at church—outside the front doors of the church in warm weather, in the inner hallway in cold weather. As soon as she saw me, she would reach in her pocket and draw out a handful of clippings containing poetry she had found during the week. She would go over each one with me before presenting the handful to me for my keeping. It was not always great poetry, but it was a humane love for me, a concern for my learning, and a fellowship of a kindred spirit that interested *Miz* Peachy, and I shall never forget her!

I don't think I heard the word "conservative" in my growing up years. I *know* I did not hear the word "liberal." I thought everyone was pretty much the same in outlook and philosophy, as I thought everyone was about the same when it came to being poor—with just a few exceptions. And you were happy with who you were and what you had. No coveting, no lusting after others' fashions, wealth, or accumulations. Maybe television brought lust into the living room—lust of all kinds.

What we had was radio. It was H. V. Kaltenborn, Walter Winchell, and Drew Pearson reporting on the progress of our troops in World War II (all four of *Miz* Peachy's sons served in World War II and *Miz* Kimmel's only son served in Europe, and brought our town's first war-bride, a beautiful French woman to live in Kendallville). And, of course, we had the marvelous radio comedies. Of an evening, my mother would pop a batch of popcorn and put it in a long, low pan. I held the pan on my lap, sitting between my parents, with the lights turned out, and we'd listen to the radio comedies. I liked Jack Benny and Fibber McGee and Molly in particular, but my all-time favorite was Red Skelton. No lust there!

Church did have a liberal dimension—toward those less fortunate, especially those living far away, reached only by foreign missionaries. And we learned to give generously—liberally—to them. I remember hearing a missionary, who came to our church, talking about his work "under the Southern Cross." I fell in love with that phrase, and it haunts my mind yet.

The phrase had an impact on our decision in 1970 to move our family from America to Liberia, where I had been appointed Fulbright Lecturer in English. We came to love the Liberian people and have grieved for them over the past 20 years as their nation has been torn by civil war, killing, and strife. Jeanne and I volunteered to return to Liberia in the 1980s to help restore the educational program, but the State Department reported that it was unsafe, and they would not approve of any such assignment.

My ultimate goal in my Liberian work was to acquaint the world with Alexander Crummell, African-American missionary, who, between 1853 and 1873 preached and taught in and around Monrovia, Liberia, as an Episcopal missionary. I thought, and still think, Crummell to be one of the most important intellectuals regarding race and race relations to live in America.

W.E.B. DuBois wrote of Crummell in DuBois' masterpiece, *Souls of Black Folk*.[1] But in Liberia, I ran into a form of conservatism I had not encountered before: I was prohibited from using the national archives—because I was white.

The conservatism of my early years was non-discriminatory, and I came to appreciate conservatism in my growing up years. I celebrate conservatism now, for it has given me a marvelous, fifty-year marriage, a splendid family, and financial stability of which I would never have dreamed as a young person. But I fear for my country when so many children grow up without loving parents in stable homes, where happy, gentle ways are celebrated on a daily basis. I fear for my country when I hear children not being immersed from their earliest years in the great literature of Western Civilization. I fear for my country for the brazen grasping of huge sums of wealth by corporate icons just because they are placed next to the indiscriminating seats of power, their corporate boards. And I fear for my country when the opportunity for children and young adults to step outside their conservatism and experience the exhilaration of redirecting their lives toward liberal solutions to important human and global concerns.

AMERICAN PHILOSOPHIC LIBERALISM

Vernon Louis Parrington is the father of American liberalism, and he is my spiritual neighbor, having been born on August 3, 1871, in a house two blocks from where I now write, in Aurora, Illinois. When I moved to this city in 1984, no one in Aurora knew of VLP and his connection to this city. I happened to be reading Richard Hofstadter's *The Progressive Historians* at the time. Hofstadter had written of Parrington and his birth in Aurora.[2]

This knowledge drove me to the local archives and then, during the next few years, across the country to Maine, New York, Kansas, Oklahoma, Washington State, and California—in search of this important historian, whose *Main Currents in American Thought* (1927)[3] won the Pulitzer Prize for History in 1928. Parrington's unexpected death in 1929 ended a career that would have been, I believe, even more distinguished than it was in its brevity. I am pleased to say that the Aurora City Council named my street "Vernon Louis Parrington Drive" in honor of this great man.

Parrington's important gift to Americans of the 1920s was his discovery that people do not rise to conservatism—they settle into it. But people do rise to liberalism. The great events of American intellectual history, events that best define this nation, occurred when the people, naturally conservative in habit of thought and deed, were stirred by their leaders to rise to specific and necessary occasions. They rose, Parrington wrote, to resist a single church across America in what was called the "Glorious Revolution in 1680." They rose to resist the Crown of England and aristocracy in what is known as the American Revolution in 1776. And they rose to overthrow slavery in what we know as the American Civil War in 1861–65.[4]

Had Parrington lived, he would have celebrated, as well, I believe, the ongoing displays of national liberalism, further defining this great nation, as the people rose to overcome the Great Depression, as they rose to combat and defeat fascism in Europe in World War II, and as they rose to rebuild war-torn Europe through the Marshall Plan after the war. Fortunately, Jonathan Alter has written of this later period in an excellent study of the early days of the Franklin Delano Roosevelt administration in *The Defining Moment.*[5]

A product of Midwestern populism, both in Illinois and Kansas, Parrington knew first-hand the necessity of an individual's rising above established social, religious, and political thought to achieve important, new dimensions for fulfillment of the democratic promise. Liberalism is an intellectual point of view and not always a political agenda.

I live in the spirit of Parrington's view of liberalism. I celebrate liberalism, for the liberalism described by Parrington has given us a nation for which we must be both thankful and proud. But I fear for my country when I see Christian Evangelicalism striving by every means possible to achieve a "single church" status in America and have the laws and customs of the land redefined within the narrow confines of the Evangelical mindset. I fear for my country when I witness the establishment of a new "aristocracy," based on wealth, position, and birth. I fear for my country when I see the accomplishments of Abraham Lincoln and the men and women of the Civil War era relegated to a new apartheid, in which equality for all is ignored and often denied, especially in fields of economic endeavor. And I fear for my country when the splendid programs created in the Franklin Roosevelt era are dismantled and altered—not because the people are better served, but for reasons far less noble.

One of my favorite passages by Parrington occurs in his splendid essay, "Roger Williams, Seeker." Williams, the founder of the Baptist movement in America, was banished from the Massachusetts Bay Colony in 1635— in the midst of a bitter winter. Taken in by Indians, he became their friend and wrote the first book in North America on their culture. He went south to what is now Rhode Island and negotiated a purchase of land from

the Indians to establish his own Colony. Parrington
called Williams a "forerunner of Emerson and the
Concord school, discovering an indwelling God of love
in a world of materials things." [6]

Reminding one of Reinhold Niebuhr, an intellectual
descendent of Parrington, Parrington called Williams,

> A humane and liberal spirit, [who] was
> groping for a social order more generous
> than any theocracy—that should satisfy
> the aspirations of [people] for a catholic
> fellowship, greater than sect or church, village
> or nation, embracing all races and creeds,
> bringing together the sundered societies of
> [people] in a common spirit of good will. [7]

In this magnificent sentence, Parrington described the
driving force of the liberal—a "humane and liberal spirit."
He defined the ultimate goal of the liberal—a "social order
more generous than any theocracy." And he envisioned
the much-to-be-desired culmination of liberalism—a
"catholic fellowship, greater than sect or church, village or
nation, embracing all races and creeds, bringing together
the sundered societies of [people] in a common spirit of
good will." A careful study of Parrington's writings leads
me to the conclusion that this passage is, in many ways,
autobiographical. It certainly speaks for me.

What Parrington did not know—but would have been delighted if he had known—is that he was a direct descendent of Williams' close associate, Daniel Shearman, first secretary of Rhode Island, who was banished from the Bay Colony in 1637 and went to Rhode Island to work with Williams. Parrington's maternal grandmother, Eunice Sherman of Busti, Chautauqua County, New York, represents the sixth generation descendent from the original settler, Daniel.[8]

The Parrington quote could, as well, stand as a thesis for this book. Like Williams—and Parrington—having achieved so much, we remain seekers, for the next phase, a new discovery, another path along the journey toward a fully mature faith by which to live in perilous and confusing times. We desire, we labor for, we do all in our power to achieve that universal fellowship, "bringing together the sundered societies of [people] in a common spirit of good will." Nothing short of moving toward, if not achieving, that noble goal will satisfy this aging spirit.

But the impediments are great. One of the greatest is, ironically, our success in bringing about a fuller sense of equality of all people. We have given equality, I am sorry to say, to ignorance *and* intelligence, and much of what passes for public opinion in our day often derives from the lowest levels of intelligence.

In 1963, Richard Hofstadter wrote his timely study,

Anti-Intellectualism in American Life,[9] "conceived," he wrote, "in response to the political and intellectual conditions of the 1950s." Such a book might well be written of the early years of the 21st Century, plagued as well by what Hofstadter called "the atmosphere of fervent malice and humorless imbecility stirred up"[10] by those who would do all in their power to achieve and maintain political power. We are the inheritors of the accumulated anti-intellectualism, past and present, and every aspect of our society has been seriously impacted by it: our government, our universities, our religious institutions, our social institutions, and our families—even our judiciary—are negatively impacted by the spirit of anti-intellectualism. I offer *Pilgriming* as a beginning, an initial step, toward living up to the rigorous standards of intellectual life that are our legacy as 21st Century Americans.

In his witty manner, Parrington wrote in his third volume, "No people was ever saved by dumb preachers."[11] There are those who would argue that preachers cannot save people in the first place. But that misses the point. Anti-intellectualism in the 21st Century is an excuse to live in the past, to steer one's life by traditions no longer valid, and to miss the tremendous opportunities that advanced scholarship, research, and thinking can bring us—from science to faith. Parrington said it so well for us, as he discussed the days of Jonathan

Edwards, when the people faced a "decadent theology that held men's minds in its tenacious *rigor mortis*."[12]

It is important to realize that the great divide between liberal and conservative is really no longer valid in our consideration. In the first place, no one—even the most ardent supporter of either polarity—is fully liberal or fully conservative. We are blends of both. That's a small portion of the both-and viewpoint I expressed earlier. And the demands in government still call for the *rising* to liberalism's challenge and benefits. Had a government more friendly to liberalism been in place when the giant hurricane Katrina struck New Orleans, the city would have been rebuilt much more swiftly and much more successfully. The government was so moribund by its own conservatism that it could not rise to the occasion, even though the need in the city was great and the promise to rebuild immediately was made by the government.

A new paradigm is now demanded to explain the rationale of difference between reigning opponents in our government and across the nation. That paradigm involves *intellection*—the quality of mind informed, or not informed, by the highest and most advanced thinking about the world and the human role in this world. We stand in great need of another Reinhold Niebuhr, an Albert Schweitzer, a Hannah Arendt in our time, who will, by the power of his or her mind, offer us both intellectual and spiritual guidance. The call is for *integ-*

rity—wholeness—in a comprehensive understanding of the human circumstance. The big-name figures—the celebrities—of these days are inane and self-centered. Too often we worship television idols, music icons, and athletic heroes, who are hardly heroic.

Liberalism, besides being visionary and courageous, is generous. I have a very conservative friend to whom I say often, "If I were as conservative as you, we couldn't be friends—it is my liberalism that brings us together and holds us as friends." My good friend Frederick Turner reports that, "in the academic circles in which [he] move[s]," his "relative conservatism" holds him together with his more liberal friends. So there you have it: Both-and in the wider world. The potential of both genuine philosophic conservatism and true philosophic liberalism is this: To be effective, they both must be open, healthily social, and tolerant. And tolerance takes the day in Democracy! I choose to make *pilgriming* a part of the great adventure—in courage, intelligence, and tolerance—to bring peace to kindred spirits of all varieties of belief, all dimensions of persuasion, all peoples of difference.

So, you see, I am *both* "conservative" and "liberal." This both-and may, indeed, be the most significant both-and dimension of my life. I now see conservative and liberal as the *systole* and *diastole* of Democracy, the contraction and expansion of a healthy society, both necessary for the well being of a living, dynamic human organism in its beneficent relationship with itself and with other governments.

Radical Moderate Fully Explained

I have become a "Radical Moderate." Let me tell you how that term came into being. Every summer for many years, on our family vacation trip to Jekyll Island, Georgia, Jeanne and I would meet Georgia author, Eugenia Price, and her friend, Joyce Blackburn, at Alfonza's Old Plantation Supper Club on St. Simon's Island for dinner. One year, she would pick up the check; the next, I would. We met there, we always joked, to solve the problems of the world. Maybe we were doing some good, for, since our last meeting, things have deteriorated a good deal on both the national and international scenes.

Be that as it may, at our last dinner together, we were in the midst of a most serious conversation, when, in response to something Genie said, I replied, "I'm a Radical Moderate!"

"You can't be that—that's an oxymoron!" Genie exclaimed, laughing.

"You call yourself *born again*," I countered, "and that's an oxymoron too!" We all laughed.

I took a pocket notebook and pen from my pocket and drew a line on the page. In the middle of the line, I placed a large "M." On the right end I placed a "C" and on the left end I placed an "L."

"Okay," I explained. "Here is the Moderate—right in the middle—" and I touched the "M." "Here is the Conservative and here is the Liberal," and I touched the "C" and the "L." "On some things, I'm here": I touched the line an inch to the left of the "M." "On other things I am here": I touched the line an inch to the right of the "M." "On very few matters am I here or here," and I touched the "L" and the "C." "Therefore, I am a Radical Moderate!" There was great laughter expressed at my new political positioning—but no one challenged it that evening.

I would like to confess to some of my readers that I am a thorough going, die-hard Conservative. To others, I'd like to admit to being a sound and absolute Liberal. But I can do neither. Alas, to all, I declare that I am a lonely Radical Moderate, living in a both-and world, of free choice—and ultimate possibility.

The challenge in our time is well expressed, it seems to me, in the words of Reinhold Niebuhr, who may himself have been something of a Radical Moderate in his day:

> The children of light must be armed with the wisdom of the children of darkness but remain free from their malice. They must know the power of self-interest in human society without giving it moral justification.

They must have this wisdom in order that they may beguile, deflect, harness and restrain self-interest, individual and collective, for the sake of the community.[13]

And in this global village, the world is our community.

Remembering the Renaissance

America was born of the Renaissance.

This fact was brought to my attention by my good friend, R. C. Longworth, Senior Writer at the *Chicago Tribune* in 2000. Dick and I had first met by telephone in 1993, when he called my office at the Salvation Army, and we talked for more than an hour about a year-long, page-one series the *Tribune* had run on children murdered in Chicago. The editorial staff had expected that, by bringing to the public's attention details of the lives of these children, the killings would slow, if not cease.

The killings had not stopped, and Dick called to ask me, "How do you people at the Salvation Army cope with failure like this? You must deal with it all the time." I'm not certain I helped him, but that conversation was the beginning of a spiritual and intellectual bond, which we have nurtured in phone conversations, correspondence, our own writings, and occasional lunches since that time.

In the spring of 2000, he and I had lunch at our favorite meeting place, Sayat Nova, an Armenian restaurant on East Ohio Street, just off Michigan Avenue and around the corner from Tribune Tower. Our conversation led to his specialty, the old Soviet Union and Eastern European nations. He had been the Moscow correspondent for United Press International from 1965 through 1969. "I learned how to understand," he told me, "what a Soviet leader *really* meant when he said this or that. I became so skilled at comprehending the intricacies of 'Soviet-speak' that it became second nature to me. But now," he added with a smile, "I am a specialist with no place to practice my specialty."

"Why," I asked him, "are some former Soviet Bloc nations making it, and others are not? Why are places like, say, the Czech Republic or Poland doing so well, when Russia and Bosnia are not?"

"That's *the* question," he replied, "in diplomatic and scholarly circles these days." Having visited all of the Soviet Bloc nations at one time or another on assignment for the *Tribune* or UPI, he knew better than most the essential nature of each nation.

"Two factors seem important in the developing health of emerging nations these days, as I see it," he elaborated. "The first is an intellectual association with the Renaissance—some linkage to the development of the scientific traditions, the artistic achievements, the explorations, and the religious freedoms that came from that movement.

"The second is a connection to Reformation traditions, through which individuals arise to a sense of equality, in which they can say to religious leaders—and, of course, by extension, to political leaders, 'Go to Hell!' The great spiritual legacy of the Renaissance, handed down over the years, is *tolerance*," Dick elaborated. "You see, if you're up for a vote against another guy, that guy just might win, and you'll have to have a decent relationship when the election is over. So people on opposing sides learned *tolerance* toward one another through democracy."

"There is some connection, it seems to me," I told him, "between tolerance and kindness."

"You are right!" he responded. "I think they have the same common referent—freedom from bigotry and prejudice."

"What you say," I replied, "reminds me of something that architect Louis Sullivan once wrote." Sullivan is one of the heroes of Chicago's past—a great architect, famous for many Chicago buildings, including the Auditorium Building of 1887 on Congress, the magnificent Carson Pirie Scott Building of 1899 (now the Sullivan Center) at State and Madison, and Holy

Trinity Russian Greek Orthodox Church of 1901 on North Leavitt Street.

Besides his monumental Chicago architecture, Sullivan left a book—the only book I ever bought because of its title: *The Autobiography of an Idea* (1927). The *idea*, of course, is that with which we most often associate Sullivan as architect: "Form follows Function." But, as in all good books, we get more than we bargained for upon purchase. In the book, Sullivan makes a statement about democracy, which I have never read in any other source. This idea, in my opinion surpasses his architectural idea and relates to Dick's and my conversation on the Renaissance. Here is what he said:

> The implications of the Democratic Idea
> branch into endless ramifications of science,
> of art, of all industrial and social activities
> of human well-being, through which shall
> flow the wholesome sap of its urge of self-
> preservation through beneficence, drawn
> up from the roots running ever deeper
> and spreading ever finer within the rich
> soil of human kindness and intelligence.
> *For kindness is the sanest of powers, and by
> its fruits shall Democracy be known.* It is of
> the antithesis that Feudalism has prepared
> the way for kindness. *Kindness, seemingly so*

> *weak, is in fact the name of a great adventure*
> *which mankind thus far has lacked the courage,*
> *the intelligence, the grit to undertake.* Its
> manly, its heroic aspect has been unknown,
> by reasons of inverted notions of reality.
> The form of myopia is of the feudal view.[1]

Democracy makes the open mind necessary. Kindness—tolerance, if you will—makes the open mind possible. Kindness is, indeed, the "great adventure," as Sullivan said, available in our lives today. It is the ultimate fusion of Christian love and Classical respect, which the Renaissance brought into a new and beautifully secular—but very powerful—relationship.

Through kindness, the furious debate in the town meeting or on the Senate floor fuses in respect for divergent partisans when the debate is complete, the vote taken, and issues determined. Kindness drives all toward the common goal democracy has wrought.

Since that conversation with Dick Longworth, I have thought often of America's own founding and the associations present in the 1770s when America came into being. The Renaissance, that 200-year period between 1400 and 1600, brought together the Greco-Roman and the Judeo-Christian cultures into new relationships, which gave birth to what we know as Western Civilization. It is not surprising to learn that the second language of many of our founders was classical Greek. It is no accident that the architecture of early buildings in our capital, Washington, D. C., is Greek and Roman in design.

There are those who would have us think that the single most important cultural force in the founding of America was Christianity. You hear again and again: "The nation was founded as a 'christian' nation!" people proclaim. But Edith Hamilton, Classics scholar so much respected by D. Elton Trueblood, who used to speak frequently of her, wrote in her important study, *The Greek Way*, about the birth of Western Civilization in ancient Greece:

> That which distinguishes the modern world from the ancient, and that which divides the West from the East, is the supremacy of mind in the affairs of men, and this came to birth in Greece and lived in Greece alone of all the ancient world. The Greeks were the first intellectualists. In a world where the irrational had played the chief role, they came forward as the protagonists of the mind.[2]

Our founding fathers were completely conscious of the importance of the "Greek Way" in what they did in the nation's founding. Their greatest contribution to the founding may well have been the prominence of the life of the mind and the mind's supreme role in the creation of the Republic. Historian Neil Harris observed in *The Artist in American Society: The Formative Years*, that, "Before Americans made pictures, they used words."[3] These words became the alpha and omega for the success of a new form of government, forged in splendid prose, which came into being in 1776 and has endured into our own time. The printed word is indeed a legacy from the written word of the ancient Greeks, and both the beauty and endurance of their linguistic creations are attributable to the Greek influence.

Even our schools were genuinely touched by the Classical influence, for, into the early 20th Century, Latin and Greek were integral to the education of American children in both public and private schools. Contemporary American poet Robert Frost was fond of remembering that he had "four solid years of Latin and Greek and not much else."[4]

Frost told me in a conversation with him in 1962 that the American education system started downhill when educators removed Latin and Greek from the common curriculum.[5]

And, of course, early educators included the ancient languages in school curricula, not only because it is important to learn another language—it most certainly is—but because studying the ideas of the Greeks and Romans in the original languages helped children understand more deeply and thoroughly their intellectual and cultural heritage as Renaissance Americans. We ought to be on the picket lines in every city and town to force ancient languages back into public schools.

My favorite Middle East commentator, Thomas Friedman, observed often following the 9/11 attacks on America that Radical Muslim culture is a culture of death.[6] His observation reminded me of Edith Hamilton's book, first published in 1943, *The Greek Way*, which I had read thirty years ago. Hamilton's thesis is this:

> The new power of mind that marked Greece arose in a world facing toward the way of the spirit...The full effect of this meeting, the immense stimulus to creative activity given when clarity of mind is added to spiritual power, can be best realized by considering what had happened before Greece, what happens, that is, when there is great spiritual force with the mind held in abeyance.

She said, "This is to be seen most clearly in Egypt where the records are fullest and far more is known than about any other nation of antiquity." "In Egypt," she concluded, "the center of interest was the dead: The ruling world-power, a splendid empire—and death a foremost preoccupation."[7]

On the other hand, Hamilton continued, "To rejoice in life, to find the world beautiful and delightful to live in, was a mark of the Greek spirit which distinguished it from all that had gone before … The joy of life is written upon everything the Greeks left behind."[8] This spirit is the Western Classical imprint upon the life of the founding of America that is as deep as, if not deeper than, the Judeo-Christian imprint.

This may be best understood when we consider the great Galileo Galilei of Renaissance fame, called by a contemporary, "the greatest light of our time." Because Galileo's studies and publications had challenged the sacred views of the church, Dava Sobel wrote,

> Shortly before Galileo returned to Arcetri, Pope Urban had issued a companion warning to the banning of [Galileo's] *Dialogue*, outlawing the reprinting of any of Galileo's earlier books. This action ensured that Galileo's works would gradually die out in Italy, where the Holy Office exerted its greatest influence.[9]

They, of course, did not die out, and neither did the life of the mind, so much a part of ancient Greece and early America. The social, industrial, medical, and technical achievements of the American nation stand as a constant reminder of our Greek heritage and the supremacy of the mind in society.

The Medieval Church had fallen into the same mode of thinking as early ancient empires—and modern Evangelicalism. Hamilton said this of these Oriental States—which could, as well, be said of the early church and today's Evangelical sects:

> In Egypt, in Crete, in Mesopotamia, wherever we can read bits of the story, we find the same conditions: a despot enthroned, whose whims and passions are the determining factor in the state; a wretched, subjugated populace; a great priestly organization to which is handed over the domain of the intellect.[10]

The despotism of the Roman Church was broken in 1517 by Martin Luther, whose 95 Theses proclaimed the freedom of humankind from the tyranny of the priestly class and made possible the form of government cherished by the early Greeks and brought into full fruition on the North American continent in 1776.

What is so amazing is how often, and how openly, a priestly class arises and how powerfully it establishes a stranglehold on a people. In an age when priestly power, in the persons of religious and racial vigilantes among media leaders, seems to have gained unhealthy proportions, it is time to issue some new "Theses," in enunciating and defining freedom from intellectual and religious oppression, while lifting humankind—or a small portion of it—to new heights of awareness, sensitivity, and intellect.

Some New Theses to Shape a Life

Therefore, integral to *pilgriming*, I hereby propose a dozen new *Theses*, by which I choose to shape my own spiritual life as an aging, but engaged citizen and Christian. I urge each person to consider these *Theses* and *write for himself/herself a set by which each can reshape and invigorate the individual spiritual life.*

- Turn off commercial television in your home. I have a saying: "If you saw it on commercial television, it has to be bad!" The content of television is often superficial, immoral, and generally unhealthy for both adults and children. It should be avoided at all costs. Viewing television, by its very nature, is an anti-intellectual act, it seems to me.

- Create a personal reading program in which you read at least one book a week. Select for this program books from a wide range of disciplines, including history, fiction, poetry, drama, psychology, intelligence studies, mathematics, natural science, physics, chemistry, earth science, and theology (See the suggested reading list, page 171).

- Build into your life personal engagements in the fine and classical arts. Attend at least four times a year a first-class dramatic performance, an opera, the symphony, poetry readings, or sacred concerts. If you do not have such performances in the community in which you live, plan into your life trips to cities or communities where they are available. Make this a part of your budget and your personal agenda multiple times each year. Jeanne and I make at least one trip a year to Stratford, Ontario, to experience Shakespeare, and we frequently attend the Shakespeare Theater—and other theaters— in Chicago.

- Find a worship center in which the mind is honored and respected and in which fine music and the other arts are performed and made available. Make it a point to understand the liturgy of worship in depth—the hymns, scripture, the creed, and other worship elements. Take nothing for granted—and share your own insights in the community of worship and fellowship as a key participant.

- Demand in your recreational activities both beauty and intelligence. Come to understand and appreciate the elements of bodily kinesthetic intelligence and the moral demands in both professional and amateur sports and entertainment.

- Come to understand and respect the sacred nature of all of life on this planet. In hunting and fishing, do not waste, abuse, or wantonly destroy any life in the creation.

- Familiarize yourself in the many points of view about all important local, state, national, and international issues. And vote, not a part of an established "voting bloc," but vote independently, determined through careful, thorough study and consideration for the candidates that best represent the needs of your community, state, or nation.

- Accept the 11th Commandment: Love, respect, and honor children! Participate with children in healthy, significant activities, through the family, neighborhood, community, schools, and religious institutions.

- Avoid celebrity-ism. Pay no homage to any and demand that all public figures be responsible, mature, moral, and beneficial to the public good.

- Cultivate friendly, loving relationships through the neighborhood, community, and professions, reflecting your own inclinations and persuasions.

- Avoid over-indulgence of any kind. Be not addicted.

- Celebrate your personal views and philosophic inclinations by association with like-minded people in settings of camaraderie.

The Renaissance and Reformation are milestones in human cultural history through which the life of the mind, great artistic achievements, scientific advancement, and human independence came into being. We need to be reminded regularly that these four elements are the hallmark of Western Civilization, and celebrate them in worship, in study, and in life.

I recall from Walt Whitman's incomparable "Passage to India" three stanzas:

> A worship new I sing,
> You captains, voyagers, explorers, yours,
> You engineers, you architects, machinists,
> yours,
> You, not for trade or transportation only,
> But in God's name, and for thy sake, O soul.

> Passage to more than India!
> Are thy wings plumed indeed for such far
> flights?
> O soul, voyagest thou indeed on voyages
> like those?
> Disportest thou on waters such as those?
> Soundest below the Sanscrit and the Vedes?
> Then have thy bent unleash'd.

> O my brave soul!
> O farther farther sail!
> O daring joy, but safe! Are they not all the
> seas of God?
> O farther, farther, farther sail![11]

Driven by mind and nurtured by soul, ours is a journey, a pilgriming, of giant proportions yet unrealized, yet expanding. It is a journey that must be done together if it is to be done at all—not in unison but in harmony, not lock-step, but like a good jazz beat, improvised and made-up, as we move together in a new intellectual syncopation, born of intellection, kindness, and cooperative activities.

The Greeks are always with us, urging us, and guiding us. Hamilton said it so beautifully: "The Greeks came into being and the world, as we know it, began." The mind became supreme and the appreciation of all things of beauty found their beginning among the Greeks. This is their legacy—this is our inheritance.[12]

Language and Faith: Do They Ever Meet?

The word and the Word are separate and distinct.

In many ways, we as Christians worship the word and neglect the Word. Or, perhaps, it's the other way around: we worship the Word and neglect the word. Somehow, we think that we can understand the Word without coming to grips with the word. We neglect our basic education and attempt to leap from the most elementary of mindsets to an understanding of the most complex and deeply philosophic concerns of the human species.

Poetry is an art form, which forces a full understanding of the word, and I do not believe we can grasp the Word except through a thorough experience with poetry. The very concept, "And the Word was made flesh, and dwelt among us" (John 1:14) is a poetic metaphor of the highest order, and it takes a somewhat sophisticated relationship with language to understand the full implications of the meaning of this sentence.

The great difference between poets and non-poets, and particularly between, say, Robert Frost and us, is that we spend our time "on the surface;" the poet spends his time *below* the surface. But the greatest poets, as Frost was and remains, wrote in such a way that the two "surfaces" blend in so subtle a way that we enjoy both levels simultaneously, to the extent we are capable and personally in tune with the poet.

UNDERSTANDING POETRY—AND LIFE —WITH ROBERT FROST AS GUIDE

But it's a tricky business, this reading of poetry, as was illustrated so brilliantly on June 3, 1962, when my wife, our four-year-old son Jon, and I sat in the living room of the Homer Noble cabin, Ripton, Vermont, talking with Robert Frost. I said to him that day, "Mr. Frost, may I ask you some questions about your poetry?"

"Just don't make them too hard," he replied with a smile.

"In 'Death of the Hired Man,' you have these lines about Mary:

"I'll sit and see if that small sailing cloud
Will hit or miss the moon."
It hit the moon,
Then there were three there, making a
    dim row,
The moon, the little silver cloud, and she.

"My students always wonder what those lines mean," I said to him.

Quick as a wink of his bright eyes, he replied in mock sternness, "What do you want it to mean—Father, Son, and Holy Ghost?" And then more seriously but no less sternly, he said, "You English teachers read too much into my poetry. It means just what it says—no more, no less!" There are two issues of importance here, it seems to me. The first is the business of interpretation: saying that the poet's metaphor, synecdoche, or other figure of speech is the equivalent of a reader's given way of interpreting a poem. The second is his comment, almost an aside, "What do you want it to mean?" This question raises the most serious issue of all, for it suggests that the poet *knows* people read his poetry with an inherent bias and bring meanings from the poems that *they* want the poet to say.

Frost, so many years ago, established awesome guidelines for me in reading and understanding poetry. I do not take lightly the reading of and talking about poetry. And I hope what I accomplish in any discussion of poetry will be looked upon with the generous smile of the poet himself, should he return not having liked what he found in the world beyond. I fulfill a responsibility he placed upon my shoulders—or so I believe.

Let me explain what I mean: Frost and the Cotners visited away the afternoon of June 3, 1962, and it was getting late. Kathleen Morrison, Frost's personal assistant and friend, who had arranged for our visit, said we should stay no longer than a couple of hours, for Frost was tired and needed rest. Toward the end of our conversation, he inscribed our copy of his latest book, *In the Clearing*, writing "To Norma and Robert Cotner/ Welcome. Visitors/Ripton, Vt./June 3 62."

I then asked if I could take some photos of him outside. He quipped, "Just don't take me in front of a birch tree or stone wall!" The conversation continued as we walked to the yard. We talked of John Kennedy and his Inauguration, in which Frost was a major participant with the reading of "The Gift Outright."

"What do you think of *Profiles in Courage*?" I asked him.

"A great book—one every American should read," he replied. He stood facing the setting sun, arms folded across his chest. "Kennedy shows us that to achieve greatness"—and here he raised his right arm above his head and made a grasping motion with his fingers—

"we have to grasp what we call the 'Divine' and make it a part of our lives." He brought his hand to his chest and touched it. It was one of those rare, lovely moments in life. We soon bid him goodbye and headed down the mountain to our car as the shadows of the western hills gathered in the valley on that late afternoon.[1]

Hearing this narrative, Frost biographer Lawrance Thompson on April 23, 1971, told me,

> He must have trusted you greatly, for I know of only one other person he was so open with about his religious faith. I must have what you have just told me for the third volume of my biography, for I will deal with Frost's faith in that volume.

I recorded the narrative and sent it to Thompson, but, of course, he died before he finished the third volume, and R.H. Winnick, who completed it, did not get into Frost's faith to the extent Thompson would have, had he lived.[2]

But Frost's faith has been a continual preoccupation of mine for the past 40 years or so. One of the most sagacious of poets, Frost took faith seriously, as evidenced in his writing, both prose and poetry. It is my very great pleasure to participate in an annual Robert Frost Colloquium, hosted by Frost's granddaughter,

Lesley Lee Francis. She invites 20 or so scholars and friends each year to a location significant to Frost, and we spend a day talking about the poet and his poetry. In 2006, we met at the University of Virginia, Charlottesville, where an important collection of Frost materials is kept. The topic under consideration was the "Idea of Justice and Mercy in the Writings of Robert Frost." It was a delight listening to and sharing with some of the finest minds in America, as they wrestled with the issue of justice and mercy in Frost's own mind and in his poetry. A dozen poems and essays were brought to focus by the discussants throughout the day. Some felt that justice was more clearly enunciated than mercy; some felt that mercy, a qualitative matter, was illustrated best through deeds rather than through language. One person made the keen observation that the genre of poetry was insufficient for dealing with the question, and Frost wrote his two masques, *The Masque of Reason* and *The Masque of Mercy*, to better deal with the complex and very important issue. Another said Frost found language insufficient to deal with mercy, and he chose the drama to illustrate it. "You don't *argue* mercy—you demonstrate it," she added.

For six hours, we sat around a large quadrangle of tables, talking. There was no consensus at the conclusion. We each left with our own views—newly formed from the enlightenment of the day's exchange. And we met at dinner following the day's engagement, to fellowship as friends with a common interest and mutual bond—the person and poetry of Robert Frost. I personally left with the sense, brilliant as the day's conversation had been, that we had hardly begun to touch the surface of the mind of this great poet, whose own learning was immersed in the Greek and Roman classics, in the great Renaissance poets and dramatists, and in both English and European poetry. I drove from Charlottesville with a sense of awe for this great American poet, so important in our national culture.

There are a dozen poems I could cite from the Frost canon to illustrate what I pursue here, but I chose to use his important essay, "Education by Poetry," which he subtitled, "A Meditative Monologue" because it was given to the Amherst College Alumni Council, November 15, 1930. In its gently whimsical way, so characteristic of the intellect of Robert Frost, it defines and establishes the wide parameters of human education.

"How shall a [person] go through college without having been marked for taste and judgment?" he asked. And these are, he admitted, "two minimal things." There are, as well, the issues of imagination, initiative, enthusiasm, inspiration, and originality ("dread words," he called them). It is the function of poetry, "the only art in the college of arts," to fulfill these important matters. He would, he admitted, settle for "enthusiasm tamed by metaphor" as a pillar of education. He would, he confessed, be willing to make "metaphor the whole of thinking."[3]

I interrupt myself at this juncture to point out that, without the understanding of metaphor, we cannot understand Scripture. "The Lord is my shepherd; I shall not want" (Psalm 23:1) is a hollow echo without an understanding of metaphor. "I am the way, the truth, and the life" (John 14:6) is meaningless unless we understand the metaphor. "And the word was made flesh, and dwelt among us" (John 1:14) is mere verbiage without an understanding of metaphor.

My Old Schofield Reference Bible Remembered

I hold in my hands a *Schofield Reference Bible* (1945), the Bible I used in my growing up years. The leather cover is thoroughly worn and unhinged from the spine. The pages of the Bible are loose, tattered, and frayed with usage. I have read it completely through twice, and I have heavily marked it with colored pencils and made marginal notes of my thoughts regarding specific passages. I paid particular attention to the interrelation of the Old and New Testaments and between various parts of each Testament. This Bible is, indeed, a biography of my religious life in my early years. It is a testimony, as well, to the beginning of my pilgrimage and illustrates my devotion to the faith of youth. For 15 years, this book was my daily companion, my constant source of inspiration, and my schoolmaster—my taskmaster—in the faith. It represents the milk with which I was nourished in the early years of my faith. (There's a nice metaphor!)

There is a sentence in Somerset Maugham's splendid Chicago novel, *The Razor's Edge*, in which the lead character, Larry Durrell, in his search for truth discovers, "A God that can be understood is no God. Who can understand the Infinite in words?"[4] I am tempted to call that the voice of cynicism. But, upon consideration, it may be similar to what Frost was suggesting in the role and use of metaphor. Because words alone are inadequate, they must be made to stand for more than they represent in their denotive modes: we must understand their connotations, which expand and explore through the word as symbol, as metaphor.

The course of pilgriming is in this wise, it seems to me: We declare, "Jesus is Lord!" But I am a democratician and do not like the affiliation of Jesus to old-world royalty, as in the word *Lord*. Is there not some better metaphor for our time and our place with which to reference Jesus in a significant relationship? There is, and he gave it to us: "[You] are my friends" (John 15:14). I especially like that metaphor, for it puts the matter on a human level, which I can fully understand. It is coupled with the command that "We should love one another" (I John 3:11), and I particularly like that, for the world now cries out for loving one another.

And what beyond that do we have to link, to bind, us in fellowship with him and one another. A word that comes to mind is *disciple*, which derives from the Latin *discere*,[5] meaning, interestingly to this discussion, *to learn*. So we progress from pilgrim, to friend, to disciple, and culminate in a constant state of learning.

The Library and Bookstore, Taskmasters of Later Faith

The library and the bookstore have become the taskmasters of my later faith. The entrance of Chicago's Newberry Library, one of the most remarkable libraries of its kind in America, is a splendid visual metaphor for the function of the book in human life.

It appears as a richly sculpted Romanesque entrance to a tunnel, through which one is invited to proceed deeply into an unknown and unfamiliar region. Libraries are like that, if we let them be. They are entrances to the most profound deepening known to humankind. Properly used, good libraries permit us to explore vast depths of intellectual and spiritual domains never envisioned outside their walls nor available in any other social enterprise—including the electronic. Great libraries do on a large scale what great books do on a smaller scale.

Of the two hundred or so books I have read over the past several years, one stands out as supremely representative of that toward which I am driving. That book is *The God Particle* (1993) by physicist and Nobel Laureate Leon Lederman.[6] Here is a book that, without sacrificing the richness, texture, and depth of the domain, offers the non-physicist opportunity to experience the pleasure of the search for the invisible particle—the God particle.

Lederman, Director of Fermi National Accelerator Laboratory in Batavia, Illinois, from 1979 until 1989, now lives in Chicago's Hyde Park neighborhood, teaches at Illinois Institute of Technology, and fulfills his passion to empower young scholars through experiences in science by working in public schools when and wherever possible. Much of his Nobel grant has been committed to the enrichment of young minds in scientific enterprises, from the Illinois Mathematics and Science Academy, of which he is considered founder, to the public schools of Chicago, where he spends considerable time and resources working with children.

In reading *The God Particle*, I am first struck by the perspicacious mind of Lederman. With uncommon wit and unexpected grace, he takes what may be one of the most complex intellectual domains known, and brings enjoyment, if not complete understanding, to the study of electrons, protons, muons, hadrons, and their relationships in the sub-atomic realm.

He takes us on a historical tour, from Fifth Century b.c. Greece to tomorrow's scientific news. We listen in on Lederman's delightful, imaginary conversations with Democritus, when the two meet in the second floor control room of Fermilab late one night—Lederman clad in his pajamas. Democritus informs Lederman (and us) of his early theory of the "a-tom" and what it meant to the Classical world. Lederman tells him (and us) what he and his colleagues have done with the concept of the atom in the particle world of modern physics.

We meet all of the personages of Western science and learn that the movement has been from the macro- to the microcosm—from the cosmos to the quark. The brilliance of Lederman's history is that it is superbly understandable, so thoroughly readable. Galileo, Newton, Kepler, Faraday, and the whole host of scientists, who forged the world as we know it today, were his friends. Lederman knew each with such intimacy that he could even joke with them across the centuries—and give us delight in the wryness of his mind.

The intimacy increases as Lederman moves into the 1950s, when he became a significant participant in the development of modern physics, winning the Nobel Prize in 1988. What strikes me—beyond his marvelous understanding of sub-atomic physics—is the depth of his perceptions and his human understanding. A few sentences from his descriptions of Fermilab as a working laboratory will illustrate what I mean:

> Buried 30 feet beneath the prairie and describing a circle four miles around lies a stainless steel tube just a few inches in diameter…Through this ring, protons race at near-light-speed velocities to their annihilation in head-to-head confrontations with their brethren antiprotons. These collisions momentarily generate temperatures of about 10,000 trillion degrees above absolute zero, vastly higher than those found at the core of the sun or in the furious explosions of a supernova. Scientists here are time travelers more legitimate than those you'll find in science fiction movies. The last time such temperatures were "natural" was a tiny fraction of a second after the Big Bang, the birth of the universe.[7]

The journey to today has been from the outer to the inner, from the surface of things to a depth beyond which our most sophisticated optical devices can peer. A grand new kind of faith is necessary and a new kind of cooperative endeavor is required—call it *love*, if you choose. Through Lederman's vision, we may indeed have at our very doorstep the fusion of three traditional mortal enemies—science, art, and religion. There is hope in this possibility, but its fulfillment will require a vital intelligence among all people. This is the challenge for America in the 21st Century: All who would understand us must know the depth of our daring, the profundity of our pursuits, and the exhilaration of our expectations.[8]

The God-particle! What a metaphor![9] It is an attempt to name in a significant way the cosmic mystery, the creative force of the Universe as the work at Fermilab is an attempt to replicate the energies—the Energy—that brought about the creation—the Creation. In particle physics, we are dealing with a *quark*. My 1969 dictionary does not carry that word. A 2006 dictionary says a *quark* is "Any of a group of six elementary particles having electric charges of a magnitude one-third or two-thirds that of the electron, regarded as constituents of all hadrons."[10]

The word itself is taken from a scurrilous thirteen-line poem in James Joyce's *Finnegans Wake*:

> —Three quarks for Muster Mark!
> Sure he hasn't got much of a bark
> And sure any he has it's all beside the mark.[11]

Much as we may wish to separate and categorize domains of learning, they seem to fuse in spite of our tendencies to isolate and divide. How astounding! The word that serves as the basis for particle physics derives from a humorous *poem* by James Joyce! This is a perfect segue for my conclusion.

If I may return to Robert Frost: Living with poetry teaches us about *beliefs*. Frost said: "There are four beliefs that I know more about having lived with poetry." They are, a personal belief, a love belief, a national belief, and, finally, "the relationship we enter into with God to believe the future in—to believe the hereafter in."[12] Frost admitted at the outset that he was "not an advocate." He was an observer—a wise observer, I might add. He has been to the abyss, peered over the edge, and reported back his findings, without cynicism, without fear, and with nothing more than a desire to create from his observations poetry that will last, *in perpetuity*.

As a disciple, I am committed to learn—all there is to know and from the best teachers available. My discipleship is long term and in depth. It encompasses poetry and science—and everything in between. This is the suitable finale of *pilgriming*, as this old man sees it in these days.

The Arts and Faith

The invitation is to become a "pyramid-dweller."

In 1986, I came across one of the most remarkable essays I have ever read. It appeared in *Harpers Magazine*, was called "Design for a New Academy," and was written by Frederick Turner, Founders Professor of Arts and Humanities at the University of Texas in Dallas.[1]

The design for the new academy, which Turner called for in this essay, was a hierarchical structure based on the interrelatedness of all academic disciplines and their progressive and encompassing natures. Mathematics, he said, is foundational to all learning, and he placed Mathematics as the basic and broadest element of a pyramid. Mathematics moved naturally and intrinsically into Physics, the next layer in the pyramid. Physics gave birth to Chemistry; Chemistry to Biology; Biology to Anthropology; Anthropology to the Arts and Humanities; Arts and Humanities to Theology, which serves as the pinnacle of the academic pyramid Turner created. In order to understand one discipline, it is necessary to understand that—or those—upon which it rests. Theology, thus, requires the broadest knowledge and the deepest commitment to learning throughout the disciplines.

"[T]he error of the academy has been to deny, by means of its metaphors of demarcation between fields, the intimate connections, the continuous and omnipresent relevance of other fields at every stage of investigation,"[2] Turner stated. Those in education have, therefore, been satisfied to work within a single "field" of study, ignoring (at best) and denying (at worst) the existence of other disciplines. He then used a phrase that resonated in my own mind: "For those *at home in the pyramid*, nothing human is alien; indeed, nothing is alien." I finally had a name for myself: I am a *"pyramid-dweller!"*[3]

Kendallville (IN) High School, my home high school, offered essentially a classical education. I studied all of the basic and advanced fields of mathematics. In my advanced chemistry and advanced physics classes, under two of the most gifted teachers living at the time, I sat beneath the somber portrait of Harold Urey, a graduate of Kendallville High School in 1911. Urey had developed "heavy water"—water with a molecular structure of ^2H_2O, rather than the usual H_2O—for which he won the Nobel Prize in 1934. I studied Latin under a woman who had studied at the Sorbonne, and I studied English literature under one of the finest teachers anywhere, who had studied English literature in England. My American literature teacher had traveled America in pursuit of native writers, whom he loved dearly—for whom he infused in me his passion.

In college, at Taylor University, I took a bachelor's degree in biology, with a minor in English. Again, I had some of the most devout teachers alive at the time. In my Master's program, at Ball State University, I studied, again under consistently remarkable professors, programs in English and history. My Ph.D. work was in the interdisciplinary field of American Studies at America's center for this discipline, the University of Maryland and the Smithsonian Institution, with Master teachers. With this wide-ranging educational background, it is easy to see why Turner's essay was both enlightening and appealing to me.

OF AUBURNS, CORDS, AND DUESENBERGS

I had, in the years immediately preceding Turner's essay, begun studying the classic American automobiles, the

Auburn, the Cord, and the Duesenberg, as art forms and their creator as an artist. I had established a congenial relationship with Gordon Miller Buehrig, the artist who designed the 1935 Auburn, the 1936 Cord, and half ("the best half," he always said!) of the custom-built Duesenbergs built between 1929 and 1934. It was amazing to me that no one had written seriously about the automobile as art, given the importance of the automobile in American life. This is particularly interesting in light of the fact that few—very few—automobiles, both American and European, have achieved the status of art, what Buehrig had called "Hollow Rolling Sculpture," in a book by that title.[4]

I wrote Turner immediately upon reading his essay in *Harpers*, telling him of my pleasure with his essay, and I sent a copy of the essay to Leon Lederman, who was in the first years of creating the Illinois Mathematics and Science Academy, a residential public high school in Aurora, Illinois, for advanced high school students. Because of my own experience in the area of gifted education prior to coming to Aurora, I had been a part of the selection team for some of the first teachers at IMSA. I suggested to Lederman when I sent Turner's essay to him that Turner might be a good speaker for the faculty and staff at IMSA.

He agreed, and soon Turner was in Aurora as a guest lecturer for the faculty of IMSA and for a poetry reading with the students.[5] He and I became friends on that trip and have maintained contact—not as close as either of us would like to have had it—over the years. He has, in the ensuing years, become one of the important figures in American intellectual life. His books are densely rich explorations throughout the hierarchies of academe. He is the only person I know who has written an epic—*Genesis*.[6] In 1985, he published a book that would highlight his preoccupation in human studies, *Natural Classicism*. This book and much of Turner's later writing is summarized in a sentence that could well be the theme of *Pilgriming*: "We have a nature; that nature is cultural; that culture is classical."[7]

In 1995, Turner published a vitally important and quite remarkable book, *The Culture of Hope—A New Birth of the Classical Spirit*. He extended the theme and concern developed in *Natural Classicism*, but added depth and detail to the subject. It is important to understand that Turner believes the human species, by nature, is classical in our genetic inheritance. Two concerns of his research are relevant to the current study: ritual and poetic rhythm.

Turner found that ritual is a vital, revealing element of humankind, which is now just being fully explored and understood. In *Natural Classicism* he discussed ritual, which, he noted,

until the last few years, was often regarded
as little more than superstitious, repetitive,
neurotic, backward, and conservative behavior,
beneath the notice of humane scholars, and
discussed by social scientists as part of the
flummery by which the harsh economic
realities of society were disguised.[8]

Religious and anthropological studies, however,
have revealed that ritual is "increasingly considered one
of most vital, creative, and healthy activities." Through
ritual, he elaborated, society "stands back from itself,
considers its own value system, criticizes it, and engages
in its profoundest philosophical and religious commerce
with what lies outside it."[9]

Intelligent ritual in religious worship is, thus, an
important fulfillment of what is both genetic and
classical in our natures. To sit in a religious service in
which every detail of the ritual is consciously forged
by a bright mind or bright minds to relate to every
other part of the elements of worship is to know the
essence of true worship. As the elements—from the
invocation, to the hymns, through the scripture, into
the collect and unison prayers, to the sermon, and
through the benediction—build, echo, and reinforce
one another, one finds intellectual pleasure not found
in any other venue of human endeavor. Conscious,

intelligent worship lies at the heart of the demand, as human beings progress into maturity.

Turner said it so beautifully: "This is the natural order of our increasing concern, because human life, higher organisms, and human beings are closer and closer approximations to the emerging nervous system of God."[10] What a brilliant illumination of, "I will put my laws into their mind, and write them in their hearts: and I will be to them a God, and they shall be to me a people." (Heb. 8:10)

Closely related to ritual is the structured prosody of lyric poetry, which Turner and German psychophysicist, Ernst Poppel, have jointly investigated. They concluded that

> ...all human poetry possesses regular lines that take roughly three seconds to recite.... We conclude that poetic meter is a way of inducing much larger regions of the brain than the left-brain linguistic centers to cooperate in the poetic process of world construction, and that the chief techniques of that world construction is the creation and maintenance of a hierarchy of temporal periodicities which makes sense of past events and is powerfully predictive of future ones.[11]

THE POETRY OF THE HYMN IN WORSHIP

This consideration, of course, leads us to the important, but often ignored, element of Protestant worship—the singing of hymns. These may be, as Turner suggested, elemental to our human condition, a part of the evolutionary development of humankind.

The tradition of hymn singing in worship is older than Christianity, and, very early, the church adopted the practice as integral to worship. One historian reports, "And at midnight Paul and Silas prayed, and sang praises unto God: and the prisoners heard them" (Acts 16:25).

Paul, the great intellectual of his day, was unmistakable in his writings that the hymn and its singing were to do more than create a mood or set a tone in worship. To the Ephesians, he wrote of the communicative value of the hymn: "Be filled with the Spirit; speaking to yourselves in psalms and hymns and spiritual songs, singing and making melody in your hearts to the Lord" (Eph. 5:18–19).

To the people of Colossae, he enunciated the principle that the wisdom of the ages is, in part, contained in and taught through the ancient songs. Paul urged them to "Let the word of Christ dwell in you richly in all wisdom; teaching and admonishing one another in psalms and hymns and spiritual songs, singing with grace in your hearts to the Lord" (Col. 3:16).

One of the fine, modern commentators on hymns and hymnology, William J. Reynolds, wrote, "The Hebrew Psalter and the manner in which it was used were the musical heritage of the early Christians."[12] He linked the common heritage of Christians and Jews to the personal nature of God and the religious experience as communicated through tunes, which "were seemingly taught and preserved in the oral tradition only." Parts, and perhaps complete portions, of modern hymn tunes span the Judeo-Christian tradition of singing in worship.

Jesus himself maintained the ancient practice of singing in his last act with his disciples. Reynolds comments, "It is not surprising to find that, at the conclusion of the Last Supper, Christ and his disciples sang a hymn which historians believe to have been a portion of the *Hallel*, Psalm 114–118."[13]

A good modern hymnal is, thus, a complete anthology of psalms, hymns, and spiritual songs, spanning all of time in both tunes and lyrics. One of the blessings of living in the 21st Century is that the whole tradition of the hymn is as close as the hymn rack in front of us in nearly every service of worship. In fact, we hold it in our hands for a lengthy time each week. If we wish, we can share in these rich collections of the Spirit's inspiration of poets and musicians since biblical times.

The Hymn Society of America called the hymn a "lyric poem, reverently and devotionally conceived, which is designed to be sung and which expresses the worshippers' attitude toward God or God's purpose in human life."[14] One common form that the lyric poem of the hymn often takes is that of the Old English ballad stanza. The Common Meter tune (marked C.M. in hymnals) is the closest form to the ballad pattern. Each four-line stanza of Common Meter has a first and third line of eight syllables, and a second and fourth line of six syllables. Other frequently used patterns are the Short Meter (S.M.) and the Long Meter (L.M.) and their variants (with refrains and doubled) and adaptations of the Common Meter. All of these ancient tunes are intertwined with the same oral traditions that produced the ballads in early cultures. Approximately one-third of the hymns in a contemporary hymnal are written to one of the tunes from the ballad tradition.

Isaac Watts (1674–1748), considered the father of the church hymn, wrote his beautiful hymn, "O God, Our Help in Ages Past," to the Common Meter tune called "St. Anne." The first stanza illustrates the structure of this form:

> O God, our help in ages past,
> Our hope for years to come,
> Our shelter from the stormy blast,
> And our eternal home.[15]

Watts' hymn, "Jesus Shall Reign Where'er the Sun," is set to "Duke Street," a Long Meter tune, illustrative of the longer common form:

> Jesus shall reign where'er the sun
> Doth his successive journeys run;
> His Kingdom stretch from shore to shore
> Till moons shall wax and wane no more.[16]

Illustrative of another stanza form, a very unusual one, is John Henry Newman's powerful hymn, my favorite hymn, "Lead, Kindly Light," which is set to "Sandon 10.4.10.4.10.10." The first stanza appears in poetic form like this:

> Lead, kindly Light, amid the encircling gloom,
> Lead thou me on;
> The night is dark, and I am far from home;
> Lead thou me on;
> Keep thou my feet; I do not ask to see
> The distant scene: One step enough for me.[17]

The diversity of the stanza pattern in hymns is extraordinary and merits much study and attention. It is linked directly to the formation of poetry through the ages. David Erdman observed that the hymn movement, begun by Isaac Watts in the 18th Century, was:

> ... nourished—more than anyone had realized—by transfusions from [George] Herbert, [John] Donne, and other metaphysical poets; to have been brought to immense power and range by the Wesleys; and to have exerted no simple influence upon the modes and tunes of subsequent English and American poets.

William Blake and Emily Dickinson, whom he called "the solitary Puritan singer,"[18] are part of the poetic tradition of the hymn. And, in more recent times, we find Robert Frost's poetry occasionally included in today's hymnals.

In 1983, when President Ronald Reagan proposed placing nuclear warheads in outer space as a part of America's defense system, I was appalled. We had not mastered nuclear energy well on Planet Earth, and now we were planning for the pollution of the boundless reaches of outer space with nuclear dangers. My reaction to this proposal was to write a hymn, which I called, "O God of Galaxies Far-Flung." I chose my favorite hymn tune, *Greensleeves*, an ancient melody, which had accompanied pilgrims for centuries on their earthly journeys. The hymn, I hoped, would accompany today's pilgrims as they journeyed beyond the planet.

Here is the hymn, written for space pilgrims going forth into the far reaches of eternity.

O God Of Galaxies Far-Flung
(Greensleeves 8.7.8.7 with Refrain)

O God of galaxies far-flung,
We offer you our praises,
For all things that your grace has done
Through space's farther traces.

Teach us the wisdom of your realm:
That dying seeds encourage life;
That calm comes quickly after storm;
And kindness negates strife.

May we in travels far from Earth
Bear witness to you truly,
And make your peace the fullness of
A way of life that's holy.

O God of galaxies far-flung,
Illumine all our findings,
Fulfill what nations long have sung:
Make straight our endless windings.

Refrain

Joy, joy to Christ our friend,
Whom God revealed in Word made Deed;
Praise, praise to mind that gives
The boundless will to lead.

The craft of the poet in creating ideas through figurative language, which will touch the reader (or singer) at the deepest levels of one's being, is at the heart of hymn writing. The task is made more difficult because the frequent use of the hymn may indeed render it commonplace. The writer's task is to create poetry true to the faith and subtle enough to permit reverberations of meanings, which echo the vastness of the divine.[19]

A World of Art in Religious Centers

There is a world of art to be explored in relation to the faith. Let me tell you a story. In the 1970s, when my wife, our two children, and I attended the National Presbyterian Church in Washington, D.C., we always sat in the front pew of the Neo-Gothic cathedral. Pastor Louis Evans, Jr. probably took it as a compliment: The Cotners were almost always in Sunday church and always sat front and center. But it was not to be close to the preacher that we sat where we did. It was to be near the exquisite art that surrounded us there. The twenty-four magnificent stained-glass lance windows flanking the liturgical center illuminated its white Italian marble in splendor. The windows, fifty feet in height, contained not only brilliant pieces of multi-colored glass arranged in both literal and figurative designs from Scripture, but also the names of the great intellectual and spiritual leaders of the faith. From where we sat, I could read "Reinhold Niebuhr" and contemplate his monumental *The Children of Light and the Children of Darkness*, one of the great books of the 20th Century. I could read "St. Paul" and recall the opening of his essay, unmatched anywhere for its wisdom and beauty: "Though I speak with the tongues of men and angels, and have not charity, I am become a sounding brass, or a tinkling cymbal" (I Cor. 13:1).

Sitting front and center also put us near the great Aeolian-Skinner pipe organ and the church choir— always attired in scarlet Medieval robes and caps and singing like a host of angels. Ernie Liggon was the choirmaster and organist in those days. His organ postludes were miniature concerts in themselves, and most of the congregation would remain in the sanctuary following the Benediction just to hear him bring the worship experience to a stunning crescendo.

Once, the pastor's wife, Colleen Townsend Evans, a former motion picture actress, invited her good friend Marge Champion, of the Marge and Gower Champion dance team, to perform "The Lord's Prayer" in the liturgical center, and we Presbyterians experienced worship in a whole new way—not unlike what our Jewish friends undoubtedly experience in their more ancient worship: "Let them praise his name in the dance" (Psalm 149:3).

I was, in those days, a devotee of historian Henry Adams and the peculiar form of "high church," so beautifully expressed in Adams' later writings. I had studied thoroughly both *Mont-Saint-Michel and Chartres* and *The Education of Henry Adams*, and I had found in them a force that lifted me beyond the institutional faith of my youth to an appreciation of the role of art, not only in worship, but in life and culture, as well. His name belonged somewhere near the Virgin in the lance windows of our church. There is a grandeur to Adams' *Mont-Saint-Michel and Chartres* not unlike the grandeur of the edifices he described. In the book, he captured the Gothic cathedral in metaphors so intelligent that they echo through the ages and throughout the entire world of art:

> The equilibrium is visibly delicate beyond
> the line of safety; danger lurks in every stone.
> The peril of the heavy tower, of the restless
> vault, of the vagrant buttress; the uncertainty
> of logic, the inequalities of the syllogisms,
> the irregularities of the mental mirror,—all

these haunting nightmares ... are expressed
as strongly by the Gothic cathedral as though
it had been the cry of human suffering, and
as no emotion had ever been expressed before
or is likely to find expression again.[20]

Living, as we do, in this age of chaos—of "multiplicity," to use one of Adams' favorite terms—we still seek the equilibrium of which he wrote. Our task, it seems to me, is to frame in language anew and to create in reality afresh a wholeness in thought, worship, and life through which, alone, Democracy can survive and flourish. Equilibrium without integrity is impossible.

I think it not too much to ask of *pilgriming* to be the beginning of this search.

Pilgriming, Defined

If anything survives beyond death, it is the mind.

Let me introduce you to Reno Tacoma, who taught me that important possibility. He was an engineer on a steam locomotive for the Pennsylvania Railroad until he was forty years old, when he received the call to pastor. He then left his beloved steam engine and entered seminary to become a Baptist minister. I met him when he was eighty-three years old, retired from the ministry, and serving as an interim pastor across the state of Indiana.

He became the interim minister of my church in 1954, and we loved him. A tall man with a beaming face and close-cropped white hair, he always wore a three-piece blue suit, and across the vest hung a gold watch chain on which was attached a large, gold railroader's pocket watch. When he began his sermons, he would unfasten the pocket watch and lay it open beside his sermon. If ever—and it didn't happen very often—his sermon ran longer that 20 minutes, he would stop speaking, smile, and say, "The train's always on time! I see my time is up; I'll finish this another time." He'd close the watch, reattach it to the chain, and bring the service to a conclusion.

In one of his sermons, which I remember so distinctly from more than fifty years ago, he said something from the pulpit on Sunday that was very un-Baptist—and I have never heard it from any pulpit since. Speaking of the afterlife, he said, "If anything of my being survives death, it will be the mind, and I do all in my power to enhance the mind every day of my life."

I mark that Sunday morning in a small Baptist church in northern Indiana as the beginning of an intellectual pursuit, which has grown and intensified over the years. Therefore, you can imagine how pleased I was to learn from a dear friend, poet Laurel Church, twenty years ago, of Hannah Arendt and her posthumous book, *The Life of the Mind*.[1] I devoured the book. I read it mornings; I read it as I drove Interstates; I read it evenings. And then I reread it. It did for me at fifty what Thoreau's *Walden* had done for me at twenty-five.

THE 'LIFE OF THE MIND' DEFINED

The Life of the Mind! If there is a more euphoric phase in the English language, I don't know what it is. What Arendt does so magnificently is trace the history of this spiritual entity—*the mind*—the birthright of all and the responsibility of every living human being. She begins with the domain of *Thinking*, an activity as ancient as the Greeks, who defined so well its parameters. This domain is that human faculty, through which a person lives richly apart from all other human beings, performs in absolute silence, and invests fully in the unseen realm. The act of thinking begins as a dialogue with the self, in which the two aspects of the person silently converse. Through the process of thinking, we become who we are and how we are identified to friends and to the world.

But Arendt takes us beyond this process most commonly associated with the mind: She introduces us to the faculty of the mind called *Willing*. The Greeks knew little of this function. It was, as Arendt so beautifully details, St. Augustine who gave to the world the intellectual faculty of willing. Arendt, who did her doctoral dissertation on the concept of love in St. Augustine, is at her finest in discussing this faculty. The intellectual process of willing carries thinking beyond the self: "This Will," she writes, "... is so busy preparing action that it hardly has time to get caught in the controversy with its own counter-will." The redemption of the will comes volitionally as the will ceases "to will and [starts] to act."[2] The natural inner conflict within the will is resolved "through a transformation of the Will itself...into Love."[3] Citing St. Paul's essay on "Love" in I Corinthians 13—"the greatest of these is love"—she defines love as "enduring and conflictless Will," which provides "weight" to the soul, "thus arresting its fluctuations."[4] I would extend that metaphor and say that *love is the ballast of the soul* in the voyage of life, giving stability and direction as we journey.

The third element in the life of the mind is *Judging*. Unfortunately Arendt died before this final portion of her book was completed. But she had written enough to reveal the direction of her thought. Emmanuel Kant is the first of the philosophers to give us judging as a component of the mind. Judging opens the mind to public scrutiny and interchange. Judging enlarges the mind, Arendt says, "through the force of imagination."[5] The imagination then leads to the "operation of reflection"—the "actual activity of judging something."[6] And, in a sense, we've come full circle—back to contemplation before action.

I don't know today whether the mind—or anything—lives in the afterlife. And you'll pardon my saying so, I don't much care: I'm neither pessimistic nor afraid. The pursuit of the life of the mind has been—and continues to be—such a grand experience. It is truly an experience without end. It now seems, that what I have become, where I have been, and where I am going are sufficient. And the great pleasure in associations with family, colleagues, friends, and fellow church folk, who share the pursuit of *Thinking*, *Willing*, and *Judging*—the life of the mind, if you will—makes life these days satisfying almost without measure. A person can ask for little more. And I consider a full, wide-ranging life of the mind as a key element in *pilgriming*.

While reading Hannah Arendt, I wrote two poems in response to her ideas, which illumine both her, and my, thinking:

SABLE FRIEND

A blackbird settled on a highway guardrail,
broad wings tracing arcs in morning light.
"Good morning," I said to sable friend.
His only answer quick pierce of yellow,
and I was gone to early morning duties,
more urgent than his—less noble, perhaps:
He, being whose vision cries to be seen—
I, appearance whose glance veils all
but shadows shaping arcs of daily intent.

I Leave You, My Love

I leave you, my love,
so that I may be with you.
I walk from your elegance
as from a sunrise,
toward remembrance of you,
woven in tapestry hanging
at entrance of my home.
All comings and goings
in my private world
are thoughts clothed
in black woolen dress,
flowing to ankles, adorned
by pearl of hair and pendant.
Reason's need is love's response:
Evanescent as a kiss, though
eternal, in the mind's domain.

The Modern World Described
in "The Pity of it All"

I have a confession to make: I was pleased to leave the 20th
Century in 2000. It was a murderous, brutal, devastating
century, full of wars and atrocities, which I wanted to leave
behind. I had hoped, I had expected, that humankind had

learned that the cruelties of the Holocaust were lessons accomplished, sad events of history left behind.

And then came September 11, 2001, and the long war in Iraq, with its suicide bombings indiscriminately taking lives by the scores each day.

"The pity of it all" seems an appropriate descriptor of our age. With the blessings of unimagined progress everywhere evident in human life, particularly in the developed nations, we seem to have turned our backs on what brought us to this point and have reverted to a frame of mind we were once so intent on leaving behind.[7]

I have watched the rise of radicalism, worldwide, and I have seen the surging power of strident religious groups of all stripes. I have studied the coy acceptance of bias in society and understand how easily it develops into prejudice. I have seen prejudice subtly emerge into malice and become hatred. And I have been a witness to hatred, like a malignancy metastasizing, to become the disease of violence and destruction, both personal and social.

Beyond observations, my thinking has been informed by my reading of Amos Elon's marvelous, *The Pity of It All.*[8] This book, the history of the Jews in Germany between 1743 and 1933, begins in the fall of 1743, with the arrival of fourteen-year-old Moses Mendelssohn, frail and sickly, at Berlin's Rosenthaler Tor, "the only gate in the city wall through which Jews (and cattle) were allowed to pass."[9] We watch the rise of this young Jewish youth to become the intellectual leader in the "Age of Mendelssohn"—the "German Socrates," as he was called. His devotion to studies launched a long series of successes, making Jews and Germany nearly synonymous for the next 200 years.

We then meet Salomon Maimon, who arrived at Rosenthaler Tor in 1778. Befriended by the always-kindly Mendelssohn, Maimon became a "*Betteljude.* A mendicant, a wandering scholar 'in search of truth,' at once a genius and a wretch."[10] Kant considered him the best interpreter of Kant's works, and Goethe attempted, without success, to bring Maimon to Weimar to "become a part of his intimate circle."[11]

We begin to understand Heinrich Heine, a genius so complex and brilliant that no good biography of him exists, who fused German and Hebrew mythologies in his poetry. "No German writer," Elon says, "has ever been so German and so Jewish and so ambivalent and ironic about both." Germans and Jews were, Heine said, "Europe's 'two ethical peoples,' who might yet make Germany 'a citadel of spirituality.' "

Or just the opposite.[12]

And, of course, we meet German Jews such as Karl Marx, whose legacy marred the 20th Century, Albert Einstein, who gave us modern science, and Hannah Arendt, whose presence nurtured America until her death in 1975.

After presenting the important Jewish personages in Germany, Elon concludes his essential study with a description of the evening in May 1933, at the Bebel-Platz, near the Brandenburg Gate, when Joseph Goebbels, under orders of the recently investitured Adolph Hitler, held the first book burning. Not only would they destroy the people whom they hated; they would also destroy their memory.

The rest, as the saying goes, is history.

A perceptive passage about the beginning of the American Civil War, from Carl Sandburg's *Abraham Lincoln: The War Years*, Vol. I (1939) seems appropriate here:

> Thus the war of words was over and the naked test by steel weapons, so long foretold, was at last to begin. It happened before in other countries among other people bewildered by economic necessity, by the mob oratory of politicians and editors, by the ignorance of the educated classes, by the greed of the propertied classes, by elemental instincts touching race and religion, *by the capacity of many men, women, and children for hating and fearing what they do not understand while believing they do understand completely and perfectly what no one understands except tentatively and hazardously.*[13]

The pity of it all in our time emerges from our failure, with so much at the very tips of our minds, to know and to understand the whole of human history, to grasp the enormous devastations social and religious hatreds have brought—and continue to bring—humankind over the years. The test of our time is whether we can forge a fellowship of intellect, kindness, courage, and discipline to counter the increasingly pervasive sectarianism, self-righteousness, and malevolence of our age.

Toward Some Sort of Conclusion of the Matter

The great Jesuit poet, Gerard Manley Hopkins (1844–1889), invented a word for what I am driving at in this study. He gave us "inscape."[14] Hopkins gave us one of the great religious poems of English literature, in which he demonstrated *inscape* and illustrated the sort of wisdom that lies at the heart of *pilgriming*. The poem, a sonnet written in 1877, goes like this:

The Windhover
to christ our lord

I caught this morning morning's minion, kingdom of daylight's dauphin, dapple-dawn drawn Falcon in his riding

Of the rolling level underneath him steady
  air, and striding
High there, how he rung upon the reign of
  a wimpling wing
In his ecstacy! then off, off forth on swing,
   As a skate's heel sweeps smooth in a bow-
      bend: the hurl and gliding
   Rebuffed the big wind. My heart in hiding
Stirred for a bird,—the achieve of, the
  mastery of the thing!

Brute beauty and valour and act, oh, air,
  pride, plume, here
   Buckle! And the fire that breaks from
      thee then, a billion
Times told lovelier, more dangerous, O
  my chevalier!

No wonder of it: sheer plod makes
  plough down sillion
Shine, and blue-bleak embers, ah my dear.
Fall, gall themselves, and gash gold
  vermilion.[15]

Hopkins wrote his poetry as a part of his personal
devotional life, and his collected poems were not published until 1918—twenty-nine years after his death.

We have here an important poet, heralded only posthumously, great in his own gifts and devoted completely and humbly to Christ his Lord. What is remarkable about this poem is that, even though it is considered one of the great religious poems of English literature, there is nothing religious in the language of the poem. It is illustrative of the subtlety that lies at the heart of the mature religious intellect.

The poem begins in the early hours of the day, when the pastor walks across plowed fields fulfilling his duties. It concludes by the fireside in the evening, when the day's work is completed, and the narrator contemplates that all things encountered throughout the day, from the hawk—the windhover—circling high in the early morning sky, to the plowed fields themselves, to the falling embers in the hearth in the evening, remind him of Christ and His encompassing love and compassion.

The poem contains echoes of Shakespeare, Homer, Plato, Clement of Alexandria, Philip Sidney, and Francis Bacon—all, without a doubt, from Hopkins' own study. It reverberates with familiar themes of Hopkins, including the circular, upward motion, the chivalric, and natural objects, captured in language so dramatically rare (I almost said *bizarre*) as to render the poem "difficult" and unlike anything composed in English literature before or after it. What we see are metaphors so intense, so powerful, that they permit mere words to express the magnificence of a poetic vision, focusing on the most important, cosmic considerations possible for humankind and making them intelligible by the human mind. Such is the continuing drama in this brief poem.

In the largest sense, this poem is a summation of one's lifespan, from youth to age. I too "caught this morning morning's minion, ... " And in writing this book, I sit by the fireside, musing on the dying coals of shifting logs—"and blue-bleak embers, ah my dear"—and contemplate truths and their implications so awesome as to be grasped only in the most subtle of metaphors—"fall, gall themselves, and gash gold vermillion."

Because the poem was not intended for mass consumption but is the poet's writing for himself (and God), it represents the finest example of Hannah Arendt's *thinking*—"a dialog with the self"—to be found anywhere in literature. Such rarity seemed, to Hopkins, to demand a new word to express and explain. He gave us that word—"inscape." It is not *land*scape, nor *sea*scape, but *in*scape. The word "landscape" has a history, which may be helpful here. It was first used in 1598 to describe Dutch paintings that presented views or vistas. The word did not appear again for thirty-four years, when it was used to describe the actual vista of an English countryside as a "landscape." Thus art informed reality.[16]

Hopkins gave us a word that may have the same power: "Inscape" is the shape, the state, and the condition of the inmost panorama of the human mind in contemplation of the Divine. Through it, we catch a glimpse of the contour of the Unseen, glance at the shape of the Invisible, come to understand in a human way something of the condition from which all emanates, has essence, and is connected. Perhaps, I might suggest, that *pilgriming* is studying the *inscape* of the human soul and making it intelligible to people of all faiths and cultures. Surely *inscape* is universal, and through contemplation of it we might achieve a degree of mutual understanding and move toward a collective motivation toward peace and good will.

James Finn Cotter, one of the best of Hopkins' critics, says this about the poem:

> "The Windhover" is dedicated "To Christ our Lord" in the same way as the poet himself is consecrated, through the gift of one's self in utter emptiness to be filled with the fullness of the Word of life, "grace after grace." The kestrel [windhover], lowest in degree of the falcon pedigree and identified as the heraldic emblem of the servant, shows the way to the hidden heart. Its soaring flight embodies the idea of gnosis, controlled action and concentration which opens to inscape of the sacrificial aim and

mark of Jesus: his lifting up above the earth in pain and glory. *One early morning in May, Hopkins caught forever the transforming life of the God-Man at work in the world and in the inner man.*[17]

This is one of the many poems I have committed to memory and often recite as I drive to work or have some need for solace in daily life, a noble reminder of the very things Hopkins knew, understood, and memorialized for us. It is a part of my intellectual superstructure in a world of trivia and sound bites. This poem constantly informs me that I adhere to no party line and subscribe to no linguistic formulae in the faith. I have achieved that rare stance of freedom—to say either "Yes!" or to say "No!"—in faith and in life. "Let this mind be in you, which was also in Christ Jesus," (Phil. 2:5) is no idle verbiage but the very essence of *pilgriming*.

Several years ago I heard the story of a ballerina whose recorded music stopped suddenly as she was performing before a large audience. In the silence of the auditorium, the dancer continued her performance as if the music were playing. Every pirouette, every leap, every turn was done to perfection, but in silence except for her soft footfalls on the stage. The audience, surprised first by the silence was stunned finally by the flawless execution of the dancer in that silence, and gave her a standing ovation when she completed the dance. Asked later how she was able to continue her dance without music, she replied, "I danced to the music in my head."

Pilgriming is dancing to the music in our heads. It is what Henry David Thoreau called, as I see it, marching to your own drummer. It is how we become "onlys"—those rare and highly important human entities, who have achieved something so singularly unique as to be distinguished from all others of the species. I suppose the question immediately arises: Does it make you happy? But that's not the important question. The important question is: Does the *only* make a positive difference in the scheme of things human? To answer the first question affirmatively is to be self-centered. To answer the second question affirmatively is to be an artist, a performer—or a disciple.

Today, I stand as an old man in Christ.

I remain committed to the person of Jesus Christ, but the Christ of today in my mind and life is far different from the Jesus of my baptismal year. I am a devotee to scripture and study in the latest translations the ideas therein expressed. But I have taken on the responsibility of knowing broadly all intellectual disciplines, from mathematics to poetry, from the arts to theology. I have attempted to integrate in as full a manner as possible the truths of learning from every discipline in this *pilgriming* enterprise.

I have found prayer to be the alignment of one's soul

with the deepest, most profound thoughts of which humankind is capable. I have found myself to be integral to a unity of nature—the cosmos, if you will—connecting me, body and soul, with all things and with the energy and culmination of every living thing, past and present. Inscape has been and continues to be a driving force in what I have called *pilgriming*.

This book has become, thus, a memoir of the *only* of my soul—a testament to one person's unique journey into the faith of age.

Endnotes

INTRODUCTION

1 Homer, *The Odyssey*, trans. Robert Fitzgerald, Garden City, NY: Doubleday & Co., Inc, 1963, pp.155-156. Fitzgerald uses the spelling, "Nohbdy" for *Nobody*.

2 Jesse Stuart, "#5," *Man with a Bull-Tongue Plow*, New York: E.P. Dutton, 1934, p. 5. See *Caxtonian* November 1999, pp. 2-3, 5 for essays about and photos of Stuart.

3 Philip Appleman, "Last-Minute Message for a Time Capsule," *New and Selected Poems, 1956-1996*, Fay-

etteville: University of Arkansas Press, 1996, p. 202. See an essay, bibliography, and photos of Appleman in *Caxtonian*, July 2001, pp. 2-3.

4 Thornton Wilder, *Our Town, A Play in Three Acts*, Acting Edition, New York: Coward-McCann, Inc., 1939, p. 83.

5 Andrew Bagnato, "A Quaker brings the word to today's college students," *Chicago Tribune*, May 1, 1987, Sec. 2, p. 6. See *Caxtonian*, December 1995, for an article about and photos of Trueblood.

6 Alfred Lord Tennyson, "Ulysses," *The Poetic and Dramatic Works of Alfred Lord Tennyson*, Boston, Houghton Mifflin Co., 1898, p. 89.

THE FAITH OF AGE

1 Harold Bloom, *Genius*, New York: Warner Books, 2002.

2 Bloom, p. 7.

3 Dava Sobel, *Galileo's Daughter,* New York: Walker & Co., 1999.

4 William Wordsworth, "Ode to the Intimations of Immortality from Recollections of Early Childhood," *The Poetical Works of William Wordsworth*, 5 vols., Oxford: The Clarendon Press, 1947, vol. IV, pp. 279-285. The passage below is from the opening of Stanza V, p. 281. The context of that phrase is so beautiful, and so appropriate to the "Faith of Youth," that I want to share the complete stanza here:

> Our birth is but a sleep and a forgetting:
> The soul that rises with us, our life's star,
> Hath had elsewhere its setting,
> And cometh from afar:
> Not in entire forgetfulness,
> And not in utter nakedness,
> But trailing clouds of glory do we come
> From God, who is our home:
> Heaven lies about us in our infancy!

5 A fuller exposition of this book and this idea appears in "Musings," *Caxtonian*, February 2000, p. 2.

6 Hannah Arendt, *The Life of the Mind*, New York: Harcourt Brace Javanovich, 1978, p. 104. (See also pp. 134-138 of this book for an elaboration of Arendt's ideas on the life of the mind.)

7 Bloom, p. 591.

8 Walt Whitman, *Leaves of Grass*, New York: Modern Library Edition, 1993, p. 95. The *Caxtonian*, August 1996 and September 2003 carried articles on Whitman.

9 Robert Frost, "The Poetry of Amy Lowell," *Robert Frost – Collected Poems, Prose, and Plays,* New York: The Library of America, 1995, p. 712.

10 Harry Emerson Fosdick, "God of Grace and God of Glory," *The Presbyterian Hymnal*, Louisville, KY: John Knox Press, 1990, p. 420.

Growing Up in a Jewish Home

1 This essay was first published in *Caxtonian*, April 1996, p. 2.

2 Pat Conroy, *Beach Music*, New York: Nan A. Talese, Doubleday, 1995.

3 Elisabeth Sifton, *The Serenity Prayer*, New York: W.W. Norton & Co., 2003. See *Caxtonian*, December 2003, for an essay on Sifton's book and for photos of the Niebuhr family, including Elisabeth.

4 Sifton, p. 13.

5 Sifton, pp. 45, 46, 65, 259-61, and 334.

6 Walt Whitman, *Leaves of Grass*, New York: The Modern Library, 1993, p. 235

7 In April 2007, Mark called Larry Saunders to tell Larry that he would be graduating from high school in two years, and he wanted Larry to be at his graduation as his "father." Larry called me shortly after Mark's call and said, "I couldn't tell him I wouldn't be there." Larry had been diagnosed with bone cancer and died on May 27, 2007. What a great loss for the human family!

On Becoming a Radical Moderate

1 W.E.B. Dubois, *Writings – Souls of Black Folk*, et al., New York: Library of America, 1986. Chapter 12 (pp. 512-520) is entitled, "Of Alexander Crummell." In many ways, Crummell was the spiritual father of DuBois and provided the initial vision for DuBois' great leadership.

2 Richard Hofstadter, *The Progressive Historians – Turner, Beard, Parrington*, Chicago: University of Chicago Press, 1968, pp. 349-434.

3 Vernon Louis Parrington, *Main Currents in American Thought –The Colonial Mind, 1620-1800*, and *The Romantic Revolution in America, 1800-1860*, New York: Harcourt Brace & Co., 1927. A third volume, *The Beginnings of Critical Realism in America, 1860-1920*, was published in 1930. All are now available through University of Oklahoma Press, 1987. For an essay about and photographs of VLP and his family, see *Caxtonian*, November 2001. In 1940, Lionel Trilling in *The Liberal Imagination* attacked Parrington and ended his reign as America's dominant intellectual force, "not equaled by that of any other writer of the last two decades," according to Trilling (p.15). Parrington was still being disparaged as recently as Carlin Romano, "The Fuller Brush-off—Margaret Fuller as Transcendentalist," *The Chronicle of Higher Education*, October 19, 2007, p. B13. The fact that Romano used Parrington at all, I suppose, suggests Parrington's ongoing importance in American intellectual history. In 1939, Malcolm Cowley cited Parrington's *Main Currents in American Thought* as one of the 12 *Books That Changed*

Our Minds (pp. 179-191). In 1942, Alfred Kazin, *On Native Grounds* said of Parrington's work: "it represents the most ambitious single effort of the Progressive mind to understand itself" (p. 155). In 1986, Kermit Vanderbilt, *American Literature and the Academy*, pp. 301-332, called Parrington the "foremost single architect of a total American literary history our country has seen" (p. 332).

4 For an excellent recent study of Parrington, see H. Lark Hall, *V. L. Parrington – Through the Avenue of Art*, Kent, OH: Kent State University Press, 1994.

5 Jonathan Alter, *The Defining Moment*, New York: Simon & Schuster, 2006.

6 Parrington, *The Colonial Mind*, p. 62.

7 Parrington, *The Colonial Mind*, p. 63.

8 Roy V. Sherman, "Some of the Descendents of Philip Shearman, The First Secretary of Rhode Island," University of Akron, n.d. Parrington's grandfather, James C. McClellan, Jr., married, in turn, two women, daughters of Daniel Sherman, from Busti, Chatauqua County, NY, and brought them to his

home in Bristol, IL. Both wives died, but his second, Eunice, before her death, gave birth to a daughter, Mary Louise, who was Parrington's mother. Parrington, thus, has direct lineage to Roger Williams' close associate, Philip Sherman—or *Shearman*, as he spelled the name.

9 Richard Hofstadter, *Anti-Intellectualism in American Life,* New York: Random House, 1963.

10 Hofstadter, p. 3.

11 Parrington, *The Beginnings of Critical Realism in America*, p. 137.

12 Parrington, *The Colonial Mind*, p. 151.

13 Reinhold Niebuhr, *The Children of Light and the Children of Darkness*, New York: Charles Scribner's Sons, 1944, p. 41.

REMEMBERING THE RENAISSANCE

1 Louis Sullivan, *The Autobiography of an Idea*, New York: Dover Press, 1927, p. 280 (Emphasis added). See *Caxtonian*, February 2003, pp.2-3 for an essay on Sullivan and photos of several of his Chicago buildings.

2 Edith Hamilton, *The Greek Way*, New York: W.W. Norton & Co., 1993, pp. 15-16.

3 Neil Harris, *The Artist in American Society: The Formative Years*, New York: Brazillen, 1966, p. 2.

4 *Notes by Robert Frost on His Life and Early Writings*, Amherst, MA: The Friends of The Amherst College Library, 1991, p. 9.

5 Interview between Robert Frost and Robert Cotner, June 3, 1962, Ripton, VT.

6 Thomas Friedman has written often of this idea in his columns in *The New York Times*. One column was, "The ABC's of Hatred," June 3, 2004, Sec. A, p. 27. Another was, "If It's a Muslim Problem, It Needs a Muslim Solution," July 8, 2005, Sec. A, p. 23.

7 Hamilton, p. 17.

8 Hamilton, p. 23.

9 Sobel, p. 349.

10 Hamilton, p. 15.

11 Whitman, pp. 510, 560, 554.

12 Hamilton, p. 21.

Language and Faith: Do They Ever Meet?

1 Interview between Robert Frost and Robert Cotner.

2 Interview between Lawrance Thompson and Robert Cotner, April 23, 1971, Princeton, NJ.

3 Robert Frost, "Education by Poetry," *Collected Poems, Prose, & Plays*, New York: The Library of America, 1995, pp. 717-728. The quote cited is on p. 718.

4 W. Somerset Maugham, *The Razor's Edge*, New York: Penguin Books, 1984, p. 261. Essays on Maugham appear, with photographs, in *Caxtonian*, April 1995, p. 2, and *Caxtonian*, September 1997, pp. 1, 2, 4.

5 *The American Heritage Dictionary of the English Language*, 4th Ed., New York: Houghton Mifflin Co., 2006, p. 515.

6 Leon Lederman, *The God Particle*, New York: Houghton Mifflin Co., 1993.

7 Lederman, p. 26.

8 See *Caxtonian*, December 2001, pp. 2-3. This issue contains the substance of the Lederman discussion and some excellent photos of "Fermilab—prairie cathedral, American Stonehenge."

9 *The New York Times*, August 7, 2007, p. D7. A headline proclaims this remarkable description: "What's in a Name? Parsing the 'God Particle,' the Ultimate Metaphor," in an article by Dennis Overby, which discusses Leon Lederman's use of the "God Particle" and his book;

10 *The American Heritage Dictionary*...p. 1432.

11 James Joyce, *Finnegans Wake*, New York: Penguin Books, 1999, p. 383. This was thought to be a perfect name for "quarks," for, when first discovered, there were but three. Now there are six.

12 Frost, "Education by Poetry," pp. 727-728.

THE ARTS AND FAITH

1 Frederick Turner, "Design for a New Academy," *Harpers Magazine*, September 1986, pp. 47-53.

2 Turner, p. 50.

3 Turner, p. 51.

4 Gordon Miller Buehrig, with William S. Jackson, *Hollow Rolling Sculpture: A Designer and His Work*, Newfoundland, NJ: Haessner Publishers, 1975. A discussion of Gordon Buehrig and his art appears, with splendid illustrations, in Robert Cotner, "Of Automobiles, Books, and a Genius in 'Hollow Rolling Sculpture'," *Caxtonian*, October 1997, pp. 1, 4-5, and in "Musings," p. 2.

5 Turner spoke to the faculty in the afternoon and gave a poetry reading to the students in the evening, on February 20, 1987.

6 Frederick Turner, *Genesis – An Epic Poem*, New York: Saybrook Publishing Co., 1988.

7 Turner, *Natural Classicism*, New York: Paragon House Publishers, 1985, p. 222.

8 Turner, *Natural Classicism*, p. 8.

9 Turner, *Natural Classicism*, p. 8.

10 Turner, *The Culture of Hope – A New Birth of the Classical Spirit*, New York: The Free Press, 1995, p. 230.

11 Turner, *Natural Classicism*, pp. 12-13.

12 William J. Reynolds, *A Survey of Christian Hymnody*, New York: Holt Rinehart and Winston, 1963, p. 4.

13 Reynolds, p. 4.

14 Carl F. Price, "What Is A Hymn?" *The Papers of the Hymn Society of America VI* (1937), p. 8.

15 Isaac Watts, "O God, Our Help in Ages Past," *Hymnbook for Christian Worship*, St. Louis: The Bethany Press, 1970, p. 23.

16 Isaac Watts, "Jesus Shall Reign Where'er the Sun," *Hymnbook for Christian Worship*, p. 288.

17 John Henry Newman, "Lead, Kindly Light," *Hymnbook for Christian Worship*, p. 46.

18 David V. Erdman, "Foreword," in Martha Winburn England and John Sparrow, *Hymns Unbidden*, New York: The New York Public Library, 1966, p. vii.

19 This discussion of the hymn as poetry first appeared in Robert Cotner, "Faith that Sings," *The Disciple*. November 1985, pp.19-22.

20 Henry Adams, *Mont-Saint-Michel and Chartres*, Boston: Houghton Mifflin Co., 1905, p. 383.

Pilgriming, Defined

1 Hannah Arendt, *The Life of the Mind*, New York: Harcourt Brace Jovanovich, Publishers, 1978. See Caxtonian, February 2002, for an essay on Arendt by Dr. Laurel Church, who did her dissertation on Arendt. This issue also contains other articles and photos.

2 Arendt, Vol. 2, "Willing," p. 101.

3 Arendt, Vol. 2, "Willing," p. 102

4 Arendt, Vol. 2, "Willing," p. 104.

5 Arendt, "Appendix: Judging," p. 257.

6 Arendt, "Appendix: Judging," p. 266.

7 An Associated Press article, Kirsten Grieshaber, "Berlin's biggest synagogue to reopen, beautiful anew," *Chicago Tribune,* August 31, 2007, Sec. 1, p. 15, records these chilling facts: In Germany in 2007, "All Jewish institutions—even bookstores and kosher groceries—have 24-hour police protection and stand behind barriers to guard against vandalism and terrorism. The [newly-opened] synagogue on Rykestrasse even has a police station inside." I don't know whether this high security is to give Jews in Germany peace of mind of whether the social conditions of Germany now require such security. If it is the former, the Jews must think the latter is the case. The pity of it all!

8 Amos Elon, *The Pity of It All*, New York: Henry Holt and Co., 2002. The following discussion of this book first appeared in Robert Cotner, "Musings," Caxtonian, August 2003, p. 2.

9 Elon, p. 1.

10 Elon, p. 56.

11 Elon, p. 58.

12 Elon, p. 118.

13 Carl Sandburg, *Abraham Lincoln – The War Years*, Vol. 1, New York: Harcourt, Brace & Co., 1939, p. 211. (Emphasis added.) See *Caxtonian*, October 1994, for an article on Sandburg by his daughter Helga, and *Caxtonian*, February 2004, pp. 3, 6-7, for an article on his writing and his collections at the University of Illinois.

14 James Finn Cotter, *Inscape – The Christology and Poetry of Gerald Manley Hopkins*, Pittsburgh: University of Pittsburgh Press, 1972, p. 3.

15 Gerard Manley Hopkins, "The Windhover," *Poems of Gerard Manley Hopkins*, ed. Robert Bridges, London: Humphrey Milford, 1918, p. 29. See *Caxtonian*, April 1997, pp. 1,5 for an article on Hopkins by Barbara Ballinger, a student of Hopkins and a long-time collector of his books. It also contains a photo of the poet.

16 *The American Heritage Dictionary*,...p. 984.

17 Cotter, p. 183. (Emphasis added.)

About the Cover

I first met Chicago artist, Donald E. Lindstrom, in the late summer of 1988. I had gone to his office at the National Livestock Board headquarters on Michigan Avenue, Chicago, because I had seen a painting he had done for Rotary International, showing a Salvation Army band playing in Daley Plaza. I wanted him to consider doing a Christmas card for the Salvation Army.

"What do you have in mind?" Don asked.

"I want something 'Chicago,' I want the Salvation Army presence, and I want a horse-drawn carriage somewhere in the scene," I replied. "Maybe the Water Tower and a bell-ringing group in front of it, with a cab-horse passing by," I added.

"You mean something like this?" he countered. He

chose some felt tipped markers from a rack on his desk, pulled out a sheet of white paper, and began sketching. In a few minutes, he had created a scene with the Water Tower, a horse carriage, and bell ringers. It was so delightful that I had him sign it, and my wife framed it and uses in our home every Christmas.

"That's just right!" I exclaimed, thoroughly amazed at Don's creative gifts. The sketch became the basis of one of his best works. Prints of it hang in Salvation Army offices across America, in Europe, and in Asia. It is my favorite of the dozen he did for me in subsequent years. That was the beginning of our friendship, which is best understood when you hear how my daughter describes it: "Don is the brother you never had," she once said. And she is right.

Don and I worked together for a dozen years in the annual Christmas card program for the Salvation Army, which we launched in 1988. Out of his generosity, Don donated the originals of his art to the Salvation Army Metropolitan Division on North Pulaski Street, Chicago, where they are displayed, a miniature gallery of a very special genre of art, which I call "Chicago Salvation Army Art."

My wife and I have assembled a small collection of Lindstrom art, and we have made certain our two children have their share, as well. Our children and grandchildren know Don and his wife Mary Ann as part of our extended family and consider them dear friends. And I have become something of a Lindstrom critic. Don Lindstrom paints with an international scope. The scene may be New England's Cape Cod, Puerto Vallarta, Mexico, Tokyo, Japan, or Door County, Wisconsin. His art is authentic to the chosen setting and yet consistent in his unique, lyrical vision of people and their surroundings.

Don does with art what Aaron Copeland does with music: He takes the popular, the everyday, the commonplace, and infuses his extraordinary sense of color, contour, and gentle whimsy. In his art, we see what everyone sees, but through the delightful prism of Don's artistic vision.

The cover of *Pilgriming – A Journey Into the Faith of Age* is "Man in the Fog," a 1967 work Don did in watercolors. It is one of my favorites and represents so well the solitary nature of all pilgrimages. I am grateful to Don for this artistic gift and his kindness in permitting me to use this work as my cover art.

References Consulted

ANNOTATED READING LIST

Adams, Henry. *The Education of Henry Adams*. Boston: Houghton Mifflin Co., 1918.

I read this book when we were living in Liberia in 1971-72, and I fell in love with the person of Henry Adams, whom I met in these pages. I liked his intellect, his attitude toward himself, and his views of the nation and his times. There's nothing quite like this autobiography anywhere.

_____. *Mont-Saint-Michel and Chartres*. Boston: Houghton Mifflin Co., 1905.

> I couldn't find this book in Africa, and I had to await my return to the States to read it. It is a marvel, with its insights into the Medieval age, the grand architecture of that period, and the craft of the artisans who gave us the unsurpassed cathedrals of France.

Alter, Jonathan. *The Defining Moment*. New York: Simon & Schuster, 2006.

> In an era when some would diminish the importance of Franklin Roosevelt, this book restores the vital role of the man and his efforts in ending the Great Depression and launching American involvement in World War II—the virtual inventing of modern America.

American Heritage Dictionary of the English Language, The. New York: Houghton Mifflin Co. 2006.

Appleman, Philip, ed. *Darwin*. 3rd ed. New York: W.W. Norton & Co., 2001.

> Philip Appleman and I graduated from the same high school and have been close

friends for more than two decades. This book is the best summation of the work and influence of our greatest biologist, Charles Darwin, and contains, as well, a fine collection of Appleman's poetry.

———. *New and Selected Poems,* 1956-1996. Fayette-ville: University of Arkansas Press, 1996. Philip Appleman is first and foremost a poet. His poetry is, at times, witty, at times, irreverent, but always, provocative.

Arendt, Hannah. *The Life of the Mind.* New York: Harcourt Brace Javanovich, Publishers, 1978. Some of the finest and most important thinking on the mind is presented by Arendt in this highly readable and totally delightful book.

Bagnato, Andrew. "A Quaker brings the word to today's college students," *Chicago Tribune,* May 1, 1987, Sec. 2, p. 6.

Bloom, Harold. *Genius.* New York: Warner Books, 2002. This book is one of the most marvelous books of recent years. It is the great bulwark against "anti-intellectualism" in our time.

Conceived around the structure of the Kabbalah, the book presents highly readable summations of the 100 most important literary geniuses in world literature.

_____. *The Western Canon – The Books and School of the Ages*. New York: Harcourt Brace & Co., 1994. Here is a splendid study of the most important works of literature in Western Civilization by a scholar who understand them well and writes like a master.

Buehrig, Gordon Miller. *Hollow Rolling Sculpture: A Designer and His Work*, with William S. Jackson. Newfoundland, NJ: Haessner Publishers, 1975. This might be considered a "coffee-table" book; but it is much more, for it details Buehrig's artistic work in the design of American automobiles, including work on the Stutz, the Packard, and the Buick, but particularly on the Auburn, the Cord, and the Duesenberg.

Conroy, Pat. *Beach Music*. New York: Nan A. Talese, Doubleday, 1995. This poignant novel tells the tale of Jack and Shyla McCall in the crucial years

during World War II, when their native
South Carolina—and the nation—was
touched so deeply by what was happening
in Europe.

Cotter, James Finn. *Inscape – The Christology and
Poetry of Gerald Manley Hopkins.* Pittsburgh:
University of Pittsburgh Press, 1972.
This book is an excellent way to get
acquainted with Hopkins, his religious
views, and his poetry.

DuBois, W. E. B. *Writings – Souls of Black Folk, et al.*
New York: Library of America, 1986.
This book, I believe, is DuBois' masterpiece—
a "must-read" for every American. It gives
crucial history and ideas of the earliest days
of the Civil Rights work in America by one
of the true geniuses of this nation.

Elon, Amos. *The Pity of It All.* New York: Henry Holt
and Co., 2002.
This important and beautifully written
history tells of the life of the Jews in Germany,
between 1743 and 1933. The Holocaust
becomes all the more understandable—and
intolerable—through this great book.

Emerson, Ralph Waldo. *Emerson – Collected Poems &* *Translations*. New York: Library of America, 1994. The fountainhead of American intellectual thought, Emerson yet stands head and shoulders above others of our literary tradition in both poetry and prose.

Erdman, David V. "Forward," in Martha Winburn England and John Sparrow, *Hymns Unbidden*. New York: The New York Public Library, 1966, pp. vii-viii. This is a remarkable study of the hymn in history and literature. The authors show the relationship between John Wesley and George Herbert, William Blake, and John Milton. The book traces the relationship of Wesley and the Moravian hymn and worship. It reveals the connections between Emily Dickinson, Gerard Manley Hopkins, and Isaac Watt and indicates the impact of Sidney Lanier and Walt Whitman on the hymn. A splendid book!

Fosdick, Harry Emerson. "God of Grace and God of Glory," *The Presbyterian Hymnal*. Louisville, KY: John Knox Press, 1990, p. 420.

Friedman, Thomas. "The ABC's of Hatred," *The New York Times*, June 3, 2004, Sec. A, p. 27.

_____. "If It's a Muslim Problem, It Needs a Muslim Solution," *The New York Times*, July 8, 2005, Sec. A, p. 23.

Frost, Robert. *Robert Frost – Collected Poems, Prose, and Plays*. New York: Library of America, 1995. Of all of the American poets of the 20th Century, I believe Robert Frost represents best of the great poetic tradition of this country, which he extends in a Classical manner with grace and wit.

_____. Interview with Robert Cotner. June 3, 1962, Ripton, VT.

_____. *Notes by Robert Frost on His Life and Early Writings*. Amherst, MA: The Friends of The Amherst College Library, 1991.

Gardner, Howard. *Frames of Mind*. New York: Basic Books, Inc., 1983. In this book, Gardner introduces us to his theory of "multiple-intelligences." This book is the beginning point of some great reads by Gardner into his view of the mind in modern times.

_____. *Five Minds for the Future*. Boston: Harvard Business School Press, 2006.
This is Gardner's latest book on the mind. It is a part of "Leadership for the Common Good" Series and explores the "Disciplined Mind," the "Synthesizing Mind," the "Creating Mind," the "Respectful Mind," and the "Ethical Mind."

Goodwin, Doris Kearns. *Team of Rivals*. New York: Simon & Schuster, 2005.
Among the many books on Abraham Lincoln, this is, in my opinion, the best. It details Lincoln's superb interpersonal intelligence—the basis for his great success as President—and gives a first-rate summary of American history in the pre-Civil War and Civil War years.

Hamilton, Edith. *The Greek Way*. New York: W.W. Norton & Co., 1993.
Hamilton gives us the best background

available for the Renaissance founding of this nation and the dangers to democracy inherent in constant warfare.

Harris, Neil. *The Artist in American Society: The Formative Years,* 1790-1860. New York: Brazillen, 1966.
This is an important book in understanding the development of arts in early America. Harris discovers that the arts played a significant role in the "spiritual life of the nation." Early artists established a rapprochement with the clergy, who, while not fully comfortable, accepted the artist as the clergy had never before done.

Hofstadter, Richard. *Anti-Intellectualism in American Life*. New York: Random House, 1963.
This book is a study of the manner in which evangelicalism impacts the intellectual life of the nation.

Homer. *The Odyssey,* trans. Robert Fitzgerald. Garden City, NY: Doubleday, 1963.
I try to reread this important masterpiece of Western Civilization at least every two years or so. It is the unrivaled tale of

Odysseus' return home to Ithaka after the Trojan War and his reclaiming his life and family after 20 years.

Hopkins, Gerald Manley. *Poems of Gerard Manley Hopkins*, ed. Robert Bridges. London: Humphrey Milford, 1918.
This is the edition through which the world came to know Hopkins for the first time. It is owned by my friend Barbara Ballinger, who kindly let me have the privilege of reading Hopkins' poetry from its pages.

Joyce, James. *Finnegan's Wake*. New York: Penguin Books, 1999.
Get a copy of one of several "guides" to *Finnegans Wake* and read them together: the novel and the guide. It will be an experience, I can assure you. Then do the same with Joyce's *Ulysses*.

Lederman, Leon. *The God Particle*. New York: Houghton Mifflin Co., 1993.
A delightful read, written by a delightful man, whose intellect sparkles in humor, insight, and wisdom.

Longworth, R. C. *Caught in the Middle: America's Heartland in the Age of Globalism*. New York: Bloomsbury USA, 2008.

The *Chicago Tribune*'s long-time specialist in International economics, Dick Longworth turns his attention in this book to how globalism is transforming the traditional society of the Midwest. The book focuses on the intersection of economics, politics, and society—a vital perspective for our time.

Maugham, W. Somerset. *The Razor's Edge*. New York: Penguin Books, 1984.

This may be my favorite novel. Set in Chicago and in Europe, it captures the spirit of the World War I generation of young idealists struggling to find significance in the world's events in which they are caught.

McCullough, David. *The Great Bridge*. New York: Simon & Schuster, 1972.

This is McCullough's best book, and it is the finest cultural history that I have read. It captures the Roebling family, the spirit of America in the late 19th Century, and the creation of one of the great icons of American history. (And, besides that, the dust jacket—as all of McCullough's are—is designed by Auroran Wendell Minor.)

Newman, John Henry. "Lead, Kindly Light," *Hymnbook for Christian Worship*. St. Louis: The Bethany Press, 1970, p. 46.

Niebuhr, Reinhold. *The Children of Light and the Children of Darkness*. New York: Charles Scribners Sons, 1944.
This book is the product of World War II and elucidates the spirit of forgiveness in society better than any I have seen.

_____. *The Irony of American History*. New York: Charles Scribners Sons, 1952.
Niebuhr takes his theological views into a study of American history without letting those views alter the democratic intent or the integrity of our way of life.

Oliphant, Tom. *Praying for Gil Hodges*. New York: Thomas Dunn Books, 2005.
Always a baseball aficionado, I read everything on the subject (while cheering for the Cubs). This is among the very

best books on baseball because it tells the personal story of Oliphant and his family, records the exciting 1955 World Series between the Yankees and the Dodgers, and gives the details on the coming of Jackie Robinson into baseball, a signal event in American sports and social history.

Parrington, Vernon Louis. *Main Currents in American Thought*. 3 vols. New York: Harcourt, Brace and Co., 1927, 1930.
This, the first intellectual history of America, stirred the minds of Americans when it was published in 1927 as no other book had done. It won the Pulitzer Prize for History in 1928—a most deserving recognition of its importance. This landmark book remains highly readable, even today, and it is a delight to come to know the comprehensive mind of VLP.

Price, Carl F. *The Papers of the Hymn Society of America VI* (1937).

Reynolds, William J. *A Survey of Christian Hymnody*. New York: Holt Rinehart and Winston, 1963.

This book has been recently reprinted because of its importance as a fine history of Christian hymns.

Sagan, Carl. *The Varieties of Scientific Experience – A Personal View of the Search for God*, ed. Ann Druyan. New York: The Penguin Press, 2006. Sagan, one of my favorite science writers, is beautifully represented in this posthumous volume containing some of his finest writing, organized around the idea of William James' *The Varieties of Religious Experience*. This is a vital read for our time.

Sandburg, Carl. *Abraham Lincoln - The War Years*, 4 vols. New York: Harcourt Brace & Co., 1939. Carl Sandburg is one of my heroes. His Lincoln studies are monumental by all reckoning. I read his six-volume biography—3,600 pages—between June 8 and September 12, 2003. What a read!

Sherman, Roy V. "Some Descendents of Philip Shearman, The First Secretary of Rhode Island." Akron, OH: University of Akron Press, n.d.

Sifton, Elisabeth. *The Serenity Prayer*. New York: W.W. Norton & Co., 2003.

> This gentle book gives us a family history, cultural history, and national history during the years of World War II, as she recounts the creation of "The Serenity Prayer" by her father, Reinhold Niebuhr.

Smith, Jean Edward. *John Marshall – Definer of a Nation*. New York: Henry Holt & Co., 1996.

> This is among the five best biographies I have read. It captures the dramatic tensions between Marshall and Thomas Jefferson and delineates the contest between Federalist and States Righters—a debate still ongoing in America.

Sobel, Dava. *Galilio's Daughter*. New York: Walker & Co., 1995.

> This is one of the most important books to be published in the last quarter of the 20th Century. It should have won a Pulitzer Prize, but, for some reason, it did not.

Stanlis, Peter. *Robert Frost – The Poet as Philosopher*. Wilmington, DE: ISI Books, 2007.

> Peter Stanlis, a long-time friend of

Robert Frost, has written an important book detailing the poet's commitment to philosophic dualism and his deep beliefs, which shaped his life and poetry.

Stuart, Jesse. *Man with a Bull-Tongue Plow*. New York: E.P. Dutton, 1934.
Jesse Stuart, who was my dear friend, wrote this marvelous collection of 703 sonnets, which capture the simplicity, elegance, and sadness of life in the hills of eastern Kentucky.

Sullivan, Louis. *The Autobiography of an Idea*. New York: Dover Press, 1927.
This splendid little book is an autobiography of Sullivan, as well as of his great idea—or ideas.

Tennyson, Alfred Lord. *The Poetical and Dramatic Works of Alfred Lord Tennyson*. Boston: Houghton Mifflin Co., 1898.
I can think of nothing more pleasant than sitting down in an evening and reading through this marvelous collection of Victorian poetry by Lord Tennyson, one of the true masters of the art.

Thompson, Lawrance. Interview with Robert Cotner. April 23, 1971, Princeton, NJ.

Thoreau, Henry David. *Walden and Other Writings*. New York; The Modern Library, 1950.
If you want to understand American self-reliance, you must read this book. When I first read it, I was 25, and could not put it down. It is a masterpiece of personal courage and insights into nature, which has helped shape American culture.

Trueblood, D. Elton. *While It Is Day*. New York: Harper & Row, Publishers, 1974.
Of the 30-some books written by Trueblood, who was a long-time friend and mentor, this book is an excellent representation of one of the fine minds of America in the 20th Century.

Turner, Frederick. "Design for a New Academy," *Harpers Magazine*, September 1986, pp. 47-53.
Every person interested in education should read this essay.

_____. *Genesis – An Epic Poem*. New York: Saybrook Publishing Co., 1988.
This rare creation fuses the present and the past in tales of love and hope. It could be said, as Turner does in one of his lines:"Now it points/Both to the future and the redeemed past."

_____. *The Culture of Hope – A New Birth of the Classical Spirit*. New York: The Free Press, 1995.
This is a beautiful book that offers hope that we might find ourselves again as a people of a rediscovered classicism.

_____. *Natural Classicism – Essays on Literature and Science*. New York: Paragon House Publishers, 1985.
From the "The Word Art as a Human Inheritance" to "Developments in the Scientific Study of Aesthetics," this important book covers the full range of the classical tradition in the arts and sciences.

_____. *Natural Religion*. London: Transaction Publishers, 2006.
In this study, Turner focuses, in his unique manner, on the credibility of faith as expressed

in many ways through many religions. But
he also gives extraordinary insight into God,
both his history and his style.

Watts, Isaac. "Jesus Shall Reign Where'er the Sun,"
Hymnbook for Christian Worship. St. Louis: The
Bethany Press, 1970, p. 288.

_____. "O God, Our Help in Ages Past," *Hymnbook
for Christian Worship*. St. Louis: The Bethany
Press, 1970, p. 23.

Whitman, Walt. *Leaves of Grass (The "Death-Bed"
Edition)*. New York: Modern Library, 1993.
Every American needs to read from cover-to-
cover the poetic creation of Walt Whitman,
for he understood so thoroughly what it
means to be an American in this grand land.

Wilder, Thornton. *Our Town, A Play in Three Acts*,
Acting Edition. New York: Coward-
McCann, Inc., 1939.

Wills, Garry. *Henry Adams and the Making of America*.
New York: Houghton Mifflin Co., 2005.
Garry Wills is our most versatile historian.

His Lincoln book is one of the very finest; his books on Jesus, Biblical personages, and classical figures are among the very best. In this Adams book, he takes the neglected nine-volume history by Adams of the Jefferson and Madison Administrations and places Adams along side Thucydides, giving further credence to our classical heritage as a nation. Wills may be the Reinhold Niebuhr of our age.

Wordsworth, William. *The Poetical Works of William Wordsworth.* 5 vols. Oxford: The Clarendon Press, 1947.

William Wordsworth defined for us the Romantic Period and created a poetry commensurate with his definition.

Index